"The power of From Dissonance to Resonance comes from a positive perspective on the Future of Work. Despite massive change in expectations, technology, and society, Cecile reminds us that success requires a human-centric approach amidst a world of digital transformation."

–**R "Ray" Wang,** Principal Analyst & Founder, Constellation Research

"Cecile helps us think differently about our workforce, focusing on what is most important – our people and their future. We should be developing our people and workplaces to adapt to change, and truly 'care' for each other."

–**Viv Maza,** Chief People Officer, Ultimate Software

Cecile brings in a fresh perspective on the future of work, questioning current HR practices and providing new thought leadership with HR Resonance. A book every leader should read if they care to become better people leaders."

–**Holger Mueller**, Vice President & Principal Analyst, Constellation Research

"Many leaders I talk with are saying they have organizations and cultures which are suffering from dissonance. They say they have no ethos or practical roadmap to change this. Cecile provides this path, in a book that is long overdue"

–**Jeremy Scrivens**, Managing Director, The Emotional Economy at Work, University of Western Australia, St Georges College

From Dissonance **to Resonance**

Bringing Your People and Organization Into Sync

Cecile Alper-Leroux

First Published April 2019

Second Edition May 2019

ISBN-13:978-1-54397-330-3

Cover and interior text design by Jennifer Rogers

For Chris, (my love)
Natalie, (my muse)
and Luc, (my inspiration)

ACKNOWLEDGEMENTS

As is true of our most fruitful human endeavors, this book began as a conversation, born of a series of observations and questions, and as such, it is a collaborative effort. The conversation has evolved and been enriched by countless voices over several years, and I hope it continues in the future as we face increasingly rapid change in all aspects of our work lives.

As a self-identified accidental author, I never set out to write a book. But as the conversations deepened and expanded, I realized that some of my musings and findings could be valuable to a broader audience if I gathered them into a narrative. As I brought the elements of the book together, the process pushed me beyond observations towards offering potential solutions to some of our most persistent organizational challenges.

This collaboration could never have started without the relentless encouragement, dedication, and drive of my colleagues and friends Trudy Wonder, connector extraordinaire; Russ Banham, exploratory instigator; and Catherine Coto, steadfast researcher, who all convinced me to take the leap into the world of writing more extensively than I had ever considered. The book would not have been completed without the unwavering support and patience of my husband Chris Alper, who has been a sounding board, co-creator and co-conspirator.

I am immensely grateful to my constant cheerleaders, the Ultimate Software Women in Leadership community, who inspire and challenge me every day, and to my own leaders over the years, who have pushed me to think and rethink my interactions with others to create a positive environment at work. I have had the great fortune of learning from so many professionals, practitioners, experts, researchers, and leaders who have shared their ideas and insights, many of which are in these pages; and I've had the honor of exchanging thoughts and enjoying passionate discussions with so many other wonderful people as the ideas in the book coalesced and took shape.

My "HR Tribe" colleagues have always generously shared their opinions and have called me out when my ideas grew a bit outlandish, but that is what makes us better and forces us to clarify and complete our thoughts. Your contributions are embedded throughout these pages and are what keeps the world of HR infinitely interesting, changeable, and challenging. Our continued openness and shared work creates tremendous opportunity and gives me hope for the future.

Finally, I am grateful to my family; my parents who

emigrated from France more than 50 years ago and gave me a unique context in which to experience the world of work, as well as instilling in me a fearlessness that serves me daily; my siblings, who have always believed in my ability to hold a conversation under any circumstances; and my children, who have been the ultimate continuous feedback and development tool. This book should be viewed as a living conversation, and one that I hope continues within your organizations.

TABLE OF CONTENTS:

CHAPTER 1: WHAT IS RESONANCE?

And Why is it Missing From the World of Work?

res·o·nance
[rez-uh-nuh ns]
a phenomenon in which an external force or a vibrating system forces another system around it to vibrate with greater amplitude. Resonance occurs when an oscillating system is driven at a frequency which is the same as its own natural frequency.

Definitions of the term "resonance" range from the musical to the chemical, and come to us from the worlds of both psychology and physics. What unites these definitions is the notion of two entities, forces, or thoughts coming together. These two forces amplify or stabilize each other with a positive result, creating synchronization and relatability that lead to something greater. Many of us remember the incredible feeling we had as children, swinging higher and higher as we pumped our legs in rhythm with the initial swing—that is resonance. Today, we increasingly find ourselves and our workforces out of sync, that perfect swing experience lost. Much of this is due to the way work is defined and performed in the modern workplace—with technologies, tools, systems, and process flows out of tune with our natural frequencies.

I chose the term "resonance" to describe my vision of a world in which people at work can resonate with the structures, ideas, norms, and new technologies that define our work experiences.

In this book, I'll provide a way for individuals, business and people leaders, HR professionals, executives and anyone else thinking about the future of work to bring their organizations into sync with the changed workforce of a new era.

A cursory scan of web article titles, magazines, and books shows that the number of increasingly intense conversations about fostering organizational health and employees' well-being in the digital age is on the rise. In organizations of every size, leaders and HR professionals are more concerned than ever about providing their employees with work that is meaningful, inspiring, and ultimately productive.

However, many of their efforts to date have not met with widespread success, because traditional HR practices rest on a transactional understanding of the employee-employer relationship. Examples of these efforts include performance reviews designed to motivate employees that only look back at past performance, and goal-based compensation schemes over which individuals have little to no influence. For other organizations, these efforts have not yet begun—sometimes because they don't know where to start addressing concerns like automating paper processes, insuring true pay-for-performance, and fostering engagement.

In the long run, this disheartening state of affairs is dangerous to the financial health of organizations worldwide, and most importantly, to the welfare and long-term career trajectories of employees in an increasingly fluid and borderless modern global workforce.

The Current Situation

To fully understand how we came to this juncture, we need to look back at the origins of modern organizations and work structures, and examine the ideas, theories, and interpersonal expectations that gave rise to them and supported their longevity.

The workplace, the nature of work, and the types of work roles have not changed materially for decades. Growing from the factory floors of the Industrial Revolution, altered by principles of early 20th century work productivity science and cemented by the post-World War II application of hierarchical military structures, the way work is defined and the nature of work roles remain startlingly similar. In fact, the majority of HR processes involving employee performance, compensation, and career paths continue to be structured on the workforce of the past.

The dissonance between the changed nature of people and work and the operating structures and patterns of past decades becomes evident in flat employee engagement numbers, the limited effectiveness of leadership development initiatives, and diversity and inclusion programs that have not significantly altered the composition of the workforce and the long-term career outcomes of underrepresented groups of people.

This is particularly problematic when one considers we are in the midst of one of the largest global population displacements and redistributions since World War II, and in the United States, since the turn of the 20th century. The flow of displaced people is increasing both opportunities and pressure on communities and the workforce, making inclusion and the understanding of people's motives, values, and aspirations more important than ever before. Perpetuating the status quo and "otherness" when it comes to diversity and inclusion is not only impractical, it is also untenable in a resonant workplace.

At the same time, many work structures continue to be defined by antiquated notions of what it means to contribute to organizational success, focusing primarily on efficiency and productivity. These include such long-disproven concepts that people must physically be in an office to accomplish quality work, and that stack-ranking employees effectively improves organizational performance.

Companies that perpetuate outmoded work structures end up disengaging employees, leading to higher turnover. The core structures of work must be reexamined and reinvented to energize and engage tomorrow's workforce.

People Are Changing

A key factor engaging employees in the workplace is their ability to be who they truly are at work, and to freely express their "uniqueness" to leaders and colleagues. Outside the workplace, people generally feel free to be themselves. It is to the benefit of employers that this "whole" person also comes to work.

Today's new multi-generational workforce is very comfortable explicitly sharing their goals and aspirations openly—what they think about themselves, how they think about work, and how they envision their careers, pre- and post-retirement. The new entrants into the workforce also are very comfortable saying what they want from their organizations and people leaders. Current employees are planning early retirement, while others are focused on careers after retirement, with working arrangements that most organizations have not yet considered.

In the United States, for example, the newest employees in the workforce are at ease with diversity—they have grown up with, gone to school with, and lived around a more openly diverse population than any generation in American history. They are also generally familiar with the concept that HR industry leaders refer to as "inclusion," and have positive expectations of inclusion for themselves, their teammates and leaders.

Yet, many workplaces are still encumbered with biases that don't necessarily represent what is actually happening in the world around us, and that is a challenge. For these companies, definitions of identity are expanding faster than their existing workforce structures and processes can accommodate, causing tensions that disconnect people from their work.

The Nature of Work is Changing

Similar outdated conceptions confront the changing nature of work. Reorganizations and realignments continue to be the norm, and are often a reaction to poorly understood forces of change acting on the global workforce. One example is the extraordinary impact of the "gig" economy on the talent marketplace. People are much more comfortable with self-directed work, multiple simultaneous assignments, and fluid workplace loyalty as a result of experiences in the gig labor market. Organizational leaders are under pressure to understand the implications and harness this value for their business benefit.

Organizations also are calling into question how work can be done, the types of possible roles, and the nature of work itself. Workforce fluidity—the dynamic way that people define both the work they do and themselves in the context of work—is a case in point. Flex work, lateral moves, stretch assignments, job boards where people can choose their assignments, and self-selecting teams are examples of fluid work configurations that energize people in their career development, yet are rarely available in the organizations of today.

Technology Can Transform—Not Simply Automate

HR technology historically has been used to automate processes and work. It must now adapt to the changing needs of people and the changing nature of work. The digital transformation of business is combining with rapidly changing interpretations of what constitutes a productive workplace. In this environment, technology that permits a focus on people is paramount.

Machine and deep learning, natural language processing, and perceptive technologies offer the chance to look behind process and transactions to the emotions and engagement of the people in the workforce. Long-distance communications have allowed people to transmit information for decades, and mobile digital technology has liberated people to execute their tasks on a more fluid time and location basis.

Why Do It

From team member to executive, we all must begin this effort to reinvent the workplace, in earnest and in ways we have never fully considered. There is a pressing need for business leaders to understand, accept and value people as individuals with distinct identities. If we don't find a way—and I believe we can—we will continue to miss connections and engagement with employees in today's modern global workforce, squandering the opportunity to curtail the meteoric rise in job turnover across the globe.

Six in 10 millennials—the United States' largest generation at work—say they're consistently looking for new employment opportunities, according to Gallup. At the same time, the aging population is not necessarily planning for a staid retirement outside of the workforce. In fact, according to a 2017 Bank of America Merrill Lynch survey, 80 percent of retirees state that they work because they choose to and experience fulfillment from working after retirement, but they want more flexible work arrangements, not just part-time but the ability to cycle between work and leisure. The need for action is immediate, and we have a great deal of work to do.

Changing the nature of organizations to encourage gig work, flexible roles, and a fluid workforce will benefit employees, the organization itself, and the bottom line. Without adaptation, organizations that don't change will become progressively less productive, innovative and profitable. The history of business is filled with examples of household names that were once institutions, but did not adapt to a changing world.

Changing the Workplace

Is it possible to make the changes that our workforce needs, to use technology to bring out the best in people, create effective and humanizing environments, and refashion our stifling organizational processes into innovative forces that drive productivity in the global marketplace? Absolutely.

A new generation of leaders, an engaged and energized workforce, and technologies that foster a culture of inclusiveness and innovation will power this transformation. This movement does not need a huge budget or staff—just commitment from key individuals.

Here is just one benefit of the resonant workforce: Diverse teams are more innovative, according to Deloitte's 2017 Global Human Capital Trends report. All those multiple viewpoints, backgrounds and opinions coalesce into profitable—even game-changing—product and service innovations, as well as new ways of collaborating both within the organization and with customers.

Other examples of Resonant HR abound. We can lead the development of new ways to compensate employees and provide more personalized benefits. We can promote the use and configuration of technologies to make work tasks more interesting and efficient. We can also create a culture of community, instilling workplace practices that encourage people to bring more of their true selves to work. These are just the beginnings of the benefits of a resonant workplace and workforce.

CHAPTER 2: HOW WE GOT HERE

1950 Year After Year

Origins

The foundation of the modern workforce was laid during the Industrial Revolution, when the world transitioned from decentralized agriculture to urbanized industry as the primary economic driver. By the late 1800s, the Industrial Revolution had produced an economy driven by a completely different set of tools and methods to create goods. Local guilds and merchants gave way to a centralized means of production, with raw materials initially flowing in from the near countryside and eventually from across the world. However, there remained a need for a systematic method of work—a way for different talents to come together as an orchestrated unit of production.

Frederick Taylor was an engineer and business theorist who studied the work process scientifically—specifically the ways work was done, and how that affected worker productivity. Taylor showed the world that people working long hours was not as efficient as optimizing how work was performed. Productivity could increase by simplifying and standardizing job tasks. At the time, factory managers had very little contact with workers, leaving them alone to produce their assigned goods. Taylor suggested business leaders use managers to oversee groups of workers, ensuring effective collaboration, and calculating what each person produced to monitor if one worker was more productive than another. The manager role and the idea of pay for performance have their roots in Taylor's work.

Taylor focused on continuous efficiency gains. Using "time and motion" studies, he calculated the time needed to perform elements of a task, ultimately demonstrating the most efficient process. Taylor discovered certain people could work more efficiently than others, and advised managers to hire people fitting that profile, to further spread efficiency throughout a company. Businesses focused on becoming efficiently-run machines in which people served as cogs.

World War II vastly expanded the industrialized labor pool in the U.S. and all industrialized countries worldwide, but the nature of work did not materially change. In the U.S., women and people of color were needed to fill the ranks of workforces depleted by young men fighting overseas. When the veterans came home, the workforce reverted to pre-war demographics. Many women returned to "traditional" caregiver roles, but did not forget the feelings of personal fulfillment, access to higher pay, and better quality of life that working outside the home had given them.

The 50s Boom Economy

In the post-World War II era, management theorists continued to impact the workplace with a focus on cutting costs. One of the best known examples of this movement was the "Whiz Kids" who served in the U.S. Army Air Forces. Led by the visionary Tex Thornton, these young officers enhanced operations by creating Stat Control, a USAAF unit with an inventory of spare parts at each base, matching the demand for spare parts with the nearest supply. Their work saved $3.6 billion in bombs, parts, and ammunition in 1943 alone.

After the war, the Whiz Kids were hired by Ford Motor Company, and embedded the military's hierarchical management structures and charts into that organization. The company's incredible postwar growth due to more efficient and profitable operations, compelled other companies to follow their lead. In the booming postwar *Mad Men* era, the hierarchical work structure predominated in most American companies.

The same effects Western Europe had felt on business due to large-scale mobilization in World War I now became significant for the American soldiers who had been swept up in World War II. For returning American soldiers, this "command-and-control" structure felt natural, even patriotic, as they were accustomed to it from their military service. Since the workforce was almost exclusively male, particularly in management roles, this structure also conformed closely to their notions of social groupings. Everyone had a specific place in the workplace hierarchy, and implicit rules existed to guide communications and collaboration with others. Companies became highly-centralized operations. Divisions, departments and jobs were based on a person's specific background and expertise, and work was appropriately assigned, supervised and completed.

In the 1970s and 1980s, the scale and scope of business expanded across the world. Globalization gave rise to multinational corporations that sold products and services in other countries, often employing local workers and executives. Global expansion drove visions of enormous profits, but cultural relations were uneasy.

Similar frictions arose in the United States. More women and people of color joined or rejoined the workforce and demanded parity with the dominant paradigm of white male control throughout the work hierarchy. Although the U.S. government had enacted regulations in the 1960s giving all people a legal foundation to seek jobs without fear of discrimination, more subtle forces such as implicit biases remained in place.

Effect on Employees

Today, although job roles once reserved primarily for white men are now more accessible to women, people of color, and other underrepresented groups, parity has yet to be achieved. At the same time, the hierarchical structures of many organizations and business leaders' ingrained viewpoints about business process efficiency and worker motivation have changed little in the 21st century.

Regardless of the goods produced or services provided, profit generated by process efficiencies—with workers perceived as extrinsic to these aims—remains the primary consideration. Despite the passage of time and the changing nature and expectations of individuals, these antiquated management theories still permeate the fabric of most organizations and are a driver of workplace dissonance. "Orders" are handed down from senior executive leaders to middle managers, who choose and delegate tasks to employees under their supervision.

People within these work structures are increasingly inhibited by the rigidity of top-down hierarchical organizations. Going over one's direct leader's head to express ideas and creativity may be perceived as inappropriate (if not insubordinate) behavior for a member of a team, affecting career prospects. These concerns lead to employee apathy, resulting in lackluster financial performance, turnover issues, decreased productivity, and competitive sluggishness.

Labor Failings

Although labor unions have given workers a voice in negotiating improvements in wages, hours and working conditions, the hierarchy of traditional management structures persists. Even in the case of worker councils in Germany and other employee-led collectives in other countries, which are more effective in advocating for employees rights, workers are treated as a bloc rather than as individuals.

North American labor unions (and policymakers) have proven to be insufficient in coping with globalization and the impetus of companies to move their manufacturing and other business operations offshore, resulting in lost jobs in America.

Today, U.S. labor unions are defending a position with ebbing power. No longer perceived as active players in the global economy, and in no way reflecting or shaping necessary changes in the workforce, unions have largely passed into a steady state, trying to preserve their power, position and even their reason for being.

Seeing is Believing

Since the early 1980s, technology has made it increasingly possible for knowledge workers to do their jobs from any location. Yet, many business leaders continue to foster a culture of "face time," placing overblown value on the need to actually see people working, eroding trust between management and employees. The true impact on productivity of people being physically present in an office or other business facility is a topic of uneasy discussion in many organizations.

All too often, managers remain more concerned about presence—where someone is—rather than with their work quality and impact. A meta-analysis by Global Workplace Analytics indicates that while 75 percent of Canadian managers trust their employees, more than 33 percent want to directly observe employees' carrying out their work. This "disconnect" is real, and employees know it. The key to bringing people and work into sync is to thoughtfully and honestly evaluate the actual requirements of work, not just the form and function.

This would include the true impact on outcomes of working onsite or virtually, work hours, and modes of communication, among other criteria.

There is certainly value in face-to-face interactions, given the focus, clarity and camaraderie that come from proximity. However, the realities of the global business environment demonstrate that companies and people must accept the value of (and certainly the need for) remote work across geographic and time boundaries.

This acceptance of flexible work arrangements requires a different mindset among business leaders. Software company executives, for example, might complain that an empty parking lot at 5 o'clock points to a disengaged workforce, when in fact the coders could work from anywhere at any time. Rather than less productivity, the opposite could be the case, since these employees avoid time wasted in traffic and the stress of being away from their families.

The real questions executives must ponder are: Is quality work getting done? Do team members have the technology, leadership, and strategies in place to work effectively and innovatively? Are they engaged in pursuing what they consider to be meaningful work? These employee experience considerations are more likely to point to engagement or disengagement than an employee's physical presence in an office.

Compensation and Recognition

Little has changed since Frederick Taylor proposed more

pay for more work. For instance, compensation is still largely monetary. Salary and bonuses remain the primary work motivators for employees, despite countless studies indicating the "carrot and stick" reward model has significant limitations. Other studies also demonstrate that employees would be open to receiving less monetary compensation in return for more time off and better working conditions, such as closer collaborations on project teams.

Over the last 20 years, HR departments have gradually introduced employee recognition programs designed to incentivize employees to perform better. Today, as demonstrated by a 2017 WorldatWork study, three out of every four companies have such programs in place. These organizations perceive their programs as crucial to a positive employee experience, and achieving employee hiring, retention, and productivity goals. However, many recognition programs are built on old models that do little to achieve the intended purpose of motivating employees.

Organizations have also recently begun to "gamify" their recognition programs and provide other ways besides money to recognize great work. With gamification, people's natural behaviors to effectively compete and collaborate in games are tapped to attain productivity goals.

Organizations are making strides, yet more than 65 percent of employees remain disengaged or actively disengaged at work, according to Gallup's annual *State of the American Workplace* survey. The percentage of "engaged employees" has hovered in the low-30 percent range in the last three surveys—despite the widespread introduction and high cost of traditional employee recognition programs.

Obviously, there is a disconnect between current approaches to employee recognition and lasting engagement. Work is valued in much the same way that Taylor calculated it in the 1920s—a payout—that has not correspondingly produced meaningful improvements in employee engagement.

Perhaps it is time to align compensation and recognition with the employee lifecycle. Starting our first jobs out of high school or college, our need for compensation and recognition are vastly different from the needs of a young parent, a mid-career executive, a soon-to-be-retiree, or a reentrant to the workforce after an illness. Yet we consistently rely on compensation based on the volume of work performed as the primary motivator of employee engagement, rather than an appreciation for individuals during a moment in time.

Leadership

The definition and construct of a business leader also derives from military and government models. In the U.S., for instance, the country's first president was a general; consequently, the paradigm of an effective leader is perceived as someone who hands down orders and tasks, while commanding the respect of subordinates. While this model makes sense in a military context where decisive actions are a matter of life and death, it is of limited value in a growth-oriented corporate setting, where human beings need to be valued for independent, meaningful contributions.

The workforce of today (and the future) is in conflict with this highly structured, markedly conformist, industrially-engineered structure. Some companies are beginning to abandon these work modes, which is evident in the emergence of shared spaces, virtual conference rooms, and cafeterias. Physical "offices" that reinforce hierarchy are giving way to virtual arrangements, hot-desking and other flexible collaborative environments, which encourage spontaneous collaboration while respecting people's individual choices. This level of flexibility at work is what new entrants to the workforce prefer, and organizations that take heed are likely to find they have more engaged and productive employees.

But who are these new workers, and how do they differ from seasoned workers who grew up in an efficiency-at-all-costs approach workplace, within command and control organizational structures? Read on to learn the answer.

CHAPTER 3: DISSONANCE EXPOSED

Four Workplace Experiences and the Nature of Today's Workforce

People today want to be themselves, declaring their identities at work as they have defined them outside of work. They want to express their authenticity and aspirations openly in the workplace, yet are often met with subtle or explicit pushback and judgement when they do so.

Unfortunately, changes in corporate policies, work systems, and cultural norms progress more slowly than the widespread acceptance of changes in people. Myriad inequities and biases persist in workplaces, partly because individuals in positions of power have not made it a business priority to ensure that inclusion and belonging for underrepresented groups and individuals is foundational to business success.

In this chapter we will explore several examples of the realities of work for underrepresented people, and what needs to change to make work fulfilling for all people—to an organization's benefit.

Women in the Workplace

The record to date for women in business is not encouraging. While more than 75 percent of CEOs list "gender equality" as one of their top ten business priorities, women nonetheless are less likely to receive a promotion or be on a path toward leadership, according to a 2016 study by McKinsey & Company. Corporate America also promotes men at 30 percent higher rates than women during their early career stages, and entry-level women workers are significantly more likely than men to have spent five or more years in the same role, the study noted.

In another study by Pew Research Center, most Americans stated that women are indistinguishable from men with regard to key leadership traits such as intelligence and innovativeness, and surpass men when it comes to compassion and organization. Other surveys back up these findings. Gallup's "Women: Work and Life Well-Lived: How to Attract, Engage, and Retain a Gender-Diverse Workforce" study, for example, concludes that women are more engaged leaders than men, and, perhaps more importantly, employees working under women are more engaged than those working under men.

Given these various conclusions, women and men would appear to be equally qualified to run a company. Yet, there are only 24 female CEOs in the Fortune 500, as of 2018. That's a dismal just under 5 percent of the total. One could argue this is progress, as there were no women CEOs on the list 25 years ago. But in fact it is less than a year ago (when there were 32 female CEOs comprising 6.4 percent). At this glacial pace, another century will pass before women reach parity with men at the top of the corporate ladder.

Unfortunately, this discrepancy extends far beyond the ranks of the Fortune 500. The *New York Times'* 2018 Glass Ceiling Index counts and compares the number of women and men who occupy important leadership roles in American life—including politics, law, business, tech, academia, film and media. According to a 2018 *New York Times* article, there are now more men named John in the halls of American government than there are women by any name, despite the fact that men named John represent 3.3 percent of the US population and women represent 50.8 percent.

Even worse than this unequal playing field are the stark differences in how men and women employees are treated by senior executive management and peers. In her 2018 book *Brotopia: Breaking Up the Boys Club of Silicon Valley*, Emily Chang, host of *Bloomberg Technology*, peels back the ugly history that has resulted in the absence of women in tech. From unfortunate early software image model selection, to highly-toxic environments and pervasive demonization of women who voice their opinions, Chang paints an unsettling picture of the "epicenter of tech innovation and creation" for women. Further, an article in *The Atlantic* entitled "Why is Silicon Valley So Awful to Women?" examined these topics, stating that women are incorrectly assumed to be in support roles—or worse, invisible.

For instance, women routinely are asked (by men) to fetch coffee and take notes in meetings, subjected to male-delivered jokes with offensive punch lines (about women), and regularly interrupted in meetings (by men).

According to Chang, the vast majority of women in technology say they had experienced sexist interactions. These were highly-educated and highly-qualified women with skillsets very much sought after in Silicon Valley. Women are well aware of both the obvious and subtler differences between men and women. The problems emerge when these differences are assumed to automatically disqualify women—or more insidiously, exclude women—from the most complex, difficult, and critical work in the corporate world.

Men in technology have stated that women, as a gender, don't want the challenge of executive leadership, which, of course, depends on individual choice, not gender difference. Nevertheless, for the women in *The Atlantic*'s article, their gender explicitly separated them in their treatment by primarily senior male executives and colleagues.

Perhaps this imbalance explains why women are leaving the technical workforce in droves. An astonishing 56 percent are heading for the exits, right in the middle of their promising careers, according to *AnitaB.org*, whose mission is to ensure that the creators of technology mirror the people and societies who use it. Regrettably, many male CEOs in the technology sector erroneously attribute the exodus to female caregiving duties at this stage of the women's lives, when the real reasons are more nuanced.

Susan Davis-Ali, Ph.D. is a former Vice President of Organizational Transformational Programs at AnitaB.org. Susan has a theory about why women are exiting the technology industry at twice the rate of men.

"On my good days, I like to give the culture the benefit of the doubt and say that technology was an industry started by men, and that's why the culture is the way it is," she says. "It's a culture that was custom-made by men and for men without exclusionary intent. Any time a profession is started and dominated by one gender, leaders make decisions because it makes sense for the dominant gender. The culture evolves from there."

The legacy and lore of the tech industry, especially in Silicon Valley, is of men starting great companies in their garages and never sleeping, Susan says. They apparently had an uncanny ability to work around the clock—glorified today as the "tech hustle."

While I have no knowledge of the family responsibilities these pioneering men may have juggled at the time, the perception is that they worked 24/7. Working on such a non-stop basis was a badge of honor sought by all. Women entered the tech workforce later, but as the research confirms, they continue to bear the majority of family responsibilities. These gender expectations limit their ability to compete within the 24/7 model of behavior created by and pursued by men.

Susan also noted that technology companies started by men often have traditional male "toys" such as foosball tables, ping-pong tables and basketball courts installed as work perks, not that many women don't also enjoy such pastimes. But would these toys be the same in tech companies founded and overseen by women? And, as we evolve toward greater gender parity, will the workplace look and function differently?

Gender stereotypes have played out for decades, certainly since the *Mad Men* era of martini-sipping male bosses depending on secretaries to do their work. But as young entrants to the workforce become an ever-larger percentage of the whole, their steadfast interest in gender parity will eventually smash these archetypes and challenge workplace assumptions associated with differences between men and women and non-binary individuals. Or will they?

"On my not-so-kind days," says Susan, "I believe men set up the tech culture to be a personal playground where they don't want women to participate. Even if the business would benefit from the change, and all the data suggest that gender diversity drives innovation, I start to question if men really want the culture to change. Do they want to embrace the changes that gender parity would bring?"

What would it take to change the work culture to be more representative and accepting of gender differences? "Men have to buy into the idea of a greater good, which might require a new model of behavior," says Susan. "This new way of behaving has to be modeled at the top of the organization."

Another reason for the unequal treatment of women and the durability of the glass ceiling is the ingrained perception that women don't provide as much attention and time to their job responsibilities as men because of presumed caretaking responsibilities. This unsettling hypothesis derives from a major research survey led by Frances McCall Rosenbluth, Ph.D., the Damon Wells Professor of Political Science at Yale University.

According to the Yale-sponsored study, people perceived by senior management to be more capable of working around the clock are more likely to receive a promotion. These people are in large part men, since women still take on more caretaking responsibilities at home.

In most societies, this is no big surprise. The study indicates that mothers are expected to handle a disproportionate amount (65 percent) of childcare duties. What is eye-opening is the study's finding that women are just as productive as men when it comes to job performance—irrespective of their work availability.

According to the study, respondents were 36 percent more likely to recommend for promotion a candidate who could be available to work at any time, including nights and weekends. "Given the disproportionate burden for family work that women bear in most societies, the requirement to be available around the clock can be as starkly negative for women as if employers were biased against women," the study states.

Yet when shown productivity data for the candidates, the respondents "no longer put much weight on availability." Time availability was not a major contributor to productivity. Rather, it was a "cheap proxy" for worker evaluations, "costly not only to women, but also to men who may prefer a better career-family or work-life balance," the study states.

"Women are in an impossible position, stuck between workplace expectations for them to be as available as men during work hours and society's expectation for them to be married with children," Dr. Rosenbluth says.

Since women are statistically more likely than men to take time off, companies use that data to protect themselves when not hiring and promoting women at the same rates as men. "In both politics and business, the thinking is that women will be more likely to interrupt their careers, slow down, and take flextime at a cost to their constituencies and employers," she explains.

While many women prefer not to have children, they are nonetheless swept into the same bucket. "Research indicates that people prefer political and business leaders both men and women—to be married with children," Dr. Rosenbluth says. "Consequently, many capable single women don't run for political office because they know voters have this expectation. Career-wise, this is a big problem."

Fortunately, there is a two-fold solution to this dilemma. The study affirms the first solution—the use of mobile, cloud-enabled, and Web-based technology that enables people to work remotely, both during and after traditional business hours. Women wanting to spend more time at home with their children can do just that and still be productive. Men with children can do the same.

The second solution is more challenging. "We as

a society must make it easier for women to balance family and career, changing the very structures and long-held beliefs about how society is organized, so women aren't the default caretakers or aren't expected to be," says Dr. Rosenbluth. "We should encourage fathers who want to be more involved in childcare by giving them the freedom to do that. Over time, this will then counter the perception that childcare is primarily a woman's responsibility."

Women Speak, Men Speak

Many women over the years have confided in me about the inequitable treatment they have experienced across their working lives and careers. When a woman forcefully speaks up at work, she is perceived as being "emotional," whereas a man doing the same is expressing "confidence." The ways in which both men and women make their points may be different, but there is no less validity in their respective opinions.

Moreover, to expand the willingness to accept parity, we need a new definition of corporate leadership that does not draw historical antecedents from male stereotypes. Many male leaders of technology companies, and of businesses in other industry sectors, are disgusted by the unequal and predatory treatment of women. They need to do more to alter the status quo—to model attitudes of fairness, respect, and equality.

Susan recalled one such boss in her career. "John had seven children and fully understood the value of spending weekends home with the kids," she says. "Yet, the company's employees would show up on Saturdays and Sundays for face time, emailing John at six in the morning to let him know they were working. John was not impressed. He was home with his family."

Pretty soon, the office was quiet on Saturdays and Sundays. John had modeled the behavior he expected of all employees. Other CEOs need to model similar attitudes. Women feel the tug of their careers pulling against their responsibilities as mothers and parental caregivers—and trust me, many of us women want that true, but ever-elusive, work-life balance. Many men feel the same way.

"Women who become successful in business and make it to the top have often felt the pressure to be men in women's clothing, figuratively speaking," Susan says. "The strength of gender diversity is lost when women feel pressured to behave in ways that are inauthentic to them. Many women feel as if natural strengths in areas such as collaboration and empathy are discounted as fluffy or soft."

Yet, empathy is what many of today's younger employees need in order to feel engaged in their work. Technology has liberated people to work where and when they feel they can be most productive, while also freeing business leaders to be more flexible in how the work is doled out. Yesteryear's hierarchical management styles are becoming irrelevant, with org charts giving way to collaboration. Employees jump from one project to another, one type of task to another, all the while learning new skills and communicating with more people across the enterprise.

"Women are incredibly gifted at individualized talent management," says Susan. "We get to know our employees, what's going on in their lives, what motivates them. There's no stigma to being too empathetic if it's framed as talent management."

Men became the predominant gender in the tech world first, but as women have joined (now representing about 22 percent of the technical workforce), the opportunity to benefit from gender diversity has increased. To borrow from Susan: on my good days, I think men did a great job creating economic solutions to social problems. Due to changes in the workforce, and aided by mobile digital technology, the old ways of leading a business are no longer the most efficient or most productive.

Running a company today is like running a family, and families prosper when they draw on everyone's strengths.

Women, as a majority of humanity, have a wide-spread long-term history of discrimination based on difference, but for some groups of people, like African-Americans in the U.S., the discrimination they continue to live with is wide-ranging, pervasive, institutionalized and insidious.

Race in the Workplace

Across the expanse of his life, Dr. Jarik Conrad has been the target of implicit bias and far worse prejudices. But he also has the wisdom to recognize his own implicit biases. Growing up in East St. Louis in a notoriously tough and largely African-American community, Jarik was a basketball standout.

"If two kids came up to us on the court wanting to join us in a game and one was black and the other white, we'd always choose the black kid since white boys can't jump," he told me laughing. "Then, I played basketball in college and realized white boys really can jump."

Jarik tells this story on the speaking circuit and it always gets its share of laughs. Then he explains what it has been like to be a talented, articulate, smart person in a black body. "It's the first thing anybody ever recognizes about me," he says. "The same thing happens to other people, based on their gender, sexual orientation, religion, and so on. Our intelligence, skillsets, humor, work ethic, and other productive personal aspects are a surprise or take a back seat to our visible differences."

Why are we all so bewildered by others' differences? Jarik has studied the phenomenon. "The brain has a default mechanism that recognizes someone different as a potential predator or adversary, which sets in motion our `flight or fight' response," he says. "When our brains are not aware of others' differences, we experience an implicit expectation that they are just like us."

This makes sense, but it does not let us off the hook when it comes to doing what is necessary to train our brains to confront the reality of daily interactions with diverse people. The challenge is to manage our own implicit biases, which are tied to culturally-ingrained stereotypes, and the similar biases of others. The latter became painfully apparent to Jarik during a recent cross-country flight. For four hours, he tried to dispel the countless stereotypes about people of color held by a Chinese national. "If you can imagine it, this individual believed these stereotypes were true of all black people," Jarik says.

Such a discussion may be inoffensive on a flight, given that Jarik and his seatmate were not likely to become fast friends. In a corporate context, however, cultural stereotypes paired with implicit bias may compel a recruiter to disqualify for employment a highly-qualified candidate of color.

Jarik shared another encounter he had with an HR leader in a workshop who says she generally didn't hire African-Americans because they were not as productive as their white counterparts, based on her experience with a former employee. When asked if she had ever worked with non-productive white employees, she responded affirmatively. Jarik commented, "If white people can have some 'bad apples,' why can't African-Americans have some bad apples too?"

It had never occurred to this individual that her bias, reinforced by a stereotype, was inappropriate to apply to everyone in a particular group. I would venture to guess we have all been guilty of such implicit biases at one time or another. "The only way to teach our brains not to experience an implicit bias is to spend significant time with people who are different from us," Jarik says.

It seems simple enough to do, but demographic data about geographic distribution tells a very different story—we tend to live with people just like us. In fact, when asked about the optimal racial make-up of a neighborhood to live in, White American respondents preferred an 80-20 white-to-black ratio, whereas Black American respondents preferred a 50-50 ratio, according to research published in the *American Journal of Sociology*.

Neurodiversity in the Workplace

The aforementioned work experiences are based on implicit biases of gender and race, resulting in on-the-spot judgments. Yet there are examples of other kinds of diversity, people whose unique perspectives and abilities would benefit the resonant workforce, if only they were accepted.

Among such individuals are those who identify as "neurodiverse," particularly people with Autism Spectrum Disorder (ASD). Neurodiversity is the next frontier in the journey toward workforce diversity and inclusion (D&I). While a great deal of work remains in the more visible realms of D&I, we must also jumpstart efforts to embrace neurological differences in the workplace.

Individuals with ASD typically experience difficulties interacting socially and interpreting verbal and nonverbal cues. They may exhibit repetitive behaviors and unusually strong sensory sensitivities. ASD as a term encompasses the truth that there is not one type of autism but many, each believed to be caused by different combinations of genetic and environmental factors.

Many people with autism tend to perceive the world differently than neurotypical people. They often have hidden strengths, such as the ability to focus intensely and recognize patterns that others don't easily see. They may have powerful attention to detail or an extensive knowledge of a particular topic, often making them experts in that subject.

Some people with autism also have sensory sensitivities, exhibiting distress in the presence of halogen lights, the texture of office furniture upholstery, and background noises from air-conditioners and heaters. By understanding these sensitivities and accommodating them in the work environment, employers can reduce discomfort for this very valuable workforce group.

Unfortunately, these unique abilities and sensitivities tend to stigmatize people with ASD in their search for work, with an astonishing 80 percent unable to secure employment, according to the advocacy group Autism Speaks. This is regrettable for them and potential employers, since more than 40 percent of ASD individuals are brilliant people like John Elder Robison. This *New York Times* best-selling author serves as Neurodiversity Scholar in Residence at The College of William & Mary, in Williamsburg, Virginia, where he co-chairs the school's neurodiversity working group. He also writes a regular blog on neurodiversity for *Psychology Today* and is a sought-after speaker on autism in education and the workplace.

Given the positive attributes of people with ASD, John believes employers are losing out in their hiring practices.

"Autistic people have been here since the beginning of time, and I think it is safe to say we've played a central role in shaping the world, insofar as the arts and sciences that move us forward," John told me. "Two hundred years ago, someone with dyslexia who could not understand words chalked on a blackboard could nonetheless learn medicine at the side of a surgeon and become a skilled practitioner of the art. Only with the rise of large-scale corporations and narrow views of employment have we become more 'disabled' than 'gifted.'"

He blames the education system in part for creating this skewed perspective. "People with autism have trouble learning because of the standardized ways of teaching that predominate in our mass-production schools," he says. "Instead of memorization and structured methods like those provided in books, we learn through intuition and experimentation. It is the transition of education to a standardized system, as opposed to the older ways of learning trades, that turned us from exceptional people into society's misfits."

The perception people often have of atypical neurological profiles like ASD is formulated by its classification as a "disorder," and for many people there is little distinction between a disorder and a mental illness. This view has fostered extreme biases and inequities. Consider that more than half (58 percent) of Americans surveyed in a 2009 study by the American Psychological Association say they would not want someone they perceived to have a mental illness in their workplace. It is no wonder that many people with ASD do not disclose their condition at work. Yet ASD is not a disorder to be cured; it's merely a variation in typical human functioning.

If an organization values outside-the-box thinking and the competitive advantages it can bring, there is no simpler solution than hiring people who think outside the box as their first instinct.

Our Differences Are Valuable

I've discussed in previous chapters how the hierarchical and conformist work structures of the mid-20th century are outdated and ineffective in today's tech-enabled, collaborative working environment. The greater the diversity of people in a company, the greater the diversity of ideas, increasing the odds that one of these concepts will make a profound business difference.

"We live in this world that values conformity, when it is our differences that provide real value," John says. "Our neurological differences make us who we are—and who we are is valuable."

People with ASD often see a solution to a technical problem hidden in plain sight to non-autistic engineers—a byproduct of their intense concentration. In fact, the 2008 financial crisis was predicted by a man with ASD who focused so deeply on mortgage statistics that he could see the market collapsing like a stack of cards, as portrayed in the 2015 Oscar-winning film, *The Big Short*. "I don't think that's something an average person would have been able to do," explained Autism Speaks spokesperson Leslie Long in a 2016 National Public Radio interview.

While people with ASD (by definition) have some degree of social difficulty, experience difficulties reading body language and unspoken cues, and engage in repetitive activities—all of which may feel strikingly off-putting in a job interview—John says these behaviors can be accommodated and mitigated.

"By and large, autistic people don't like fluorescent lights, have trouble dealing with hard, concrete walls that make a room echo, and need to take extra time in considering how to complete a task," he explains. "These are not difficult accommodations, given the value a company receives in return. You must always pay a price for something that is valuable."

In return, companies will find they have hired people who are extremely dedicated to their job. "Spending less time engaged in social activities means you have someone who will focus on a task until its completion," he says. "Mastering problems at work becomes a central preoccupation, contrasted with someone who is neurotypical and has other interests beyond work. Often this results in the person staying at the office until he or she is the last one there, happily engaged in the task the entire time until the lights turn off or fatigue sets in." He added, "I'm not saying that autistic people are better than neurotypical people, just that we're different."

Gray Benoist, a father of two sons on the spectrum, understood this so well he created a technology consulting business that specializes in hiring people who are on the spectrum. His company MindSpark (since acquired in 2018 by German company Auticon), guides managers to adjust, within reason, to their employees' unique boundaries. As Susan Dominus depicted in a 2019 *New York Times* article, "Open Office", "absences, in general, are not encouraged, but they are accepted as a cost of doing business with a population that often experiences depression."

At a level of more common neurodiversity, introverts have an uneasy time with many aspects of the dominant work culture. The corporate world is often led by and built for extroverts—an individual considered to be a "people person," who finds it easy to speak up in meetings, and enjoys team-building events like group activities. Such confident behaviors are interpreted as positive contributions, helping the person get noticed for a promotion. Not so for many introverts, for whom adapting to the most vocal and dominant expectations can be a very real challenge. The additional energy load negatively impacts their productivity and ability to be authentic at work.

Furthermore, the binary notion of having only extroverts or introverts is reductive and rarely holds true at work. Many people self-identify as ambiverts (both introverted and extroverted)—68 percent of the population, according to Barry Smith, professor emeritus and director of the Laboratories of Human Psychophysiology at the University of Maryland. Either they are the life of the party in the office, then go home and quietly recharge, or they present themselves as quiet and focused in the workplace, but are much livelier outside of work.

If we associate a specific personality type with success in a role—extroverts make the best salespeople and copy editors are always introverts—we miss out on the nuances of the majority of the population. In doing so, we fail to prepare leaders to support, manage, and coach for the variability inherent in people.

This becomes critical when considering ASD individuals for jobs. For example, recruiters may assume that the profile of an

ASD job seeker is that of a "white male math wizard introvert," and target their job marketing toward that profile. However, this practice limits the person's job opportunities in other parts of the organization. For one thing, not all ASD individuals are white men who excel at recognizing mathematical patterns. Women and people of color with ASD can also excel at public presentations or pattern recognition, but could be overlooked for a promotion due to their one-on-one conversational skills.

Regrettably, the unique challenges and capabilities of people with ASD, and the frustrating interactions of introverts in an extroverted world, are not visible to the majority of neurotypical people. What is visible are our surface differences, which have no value at all.

Intersectionality in the Workforce

Such is often the case for Deborah Dagit, whose uniqueness typically is summed up by her gender and physical dimensions. The former Chief Diversity officer is a woman and a little person. In 2013, Deb opened her own diversity consulting business because she was "plain fed up," she says, with people not seeing her as she truly is. "When I interacted with an employee who'd never met a little person before, they couldn't get through the `shock and awe' of the experience," she says. "It just made the day exhausting to have to educate others about what it was like to be a little person."

Deb suggests that business leaders emphasize the equal value of every employee's thoughts and ideas and let human nature take its course. "Spending time in conversation and engaged in projects and tasks with groups of people who are different helps many people become more comfortable with each other's differences," she explains. "But you need a regular diet of such diversity immersion experiences. It's not a 'one and done' thing to authentically appreciate and cherish each other's differences."

Deb's experience is similar to those of many other individuals who have multiple differences setting them apart from the dominant workforce demographic, each difference classifying them as a member of an underrepresented group. The compound effect of their differences increases feelings of not belonging. Researchers have a term for such people and their work experiences. Called "intersectionality," it is defined as the "interconnected nature of social categorizations such as race, class, and gender as they apply to a given individual or group, creating overlapping and interdependent systems of discrimination or disadvantage."

Although few studies delve into the unique experience of having multiple differences, what is known is that the aggregate effect can cause so-called "weathering," an accumulation of micro-aggressions, frustrations, and misunderstandings that wear a person down and lead to negative health outcomes—as revealed by Linda Villarose in a 2018 *New York Times* article, "Why America's Black Mothers and Babies Are in a Life-or-Death Crisis."

As the diversity of the global workforce increases, efforts must be undertaken to better understand intersectionality and its effect on work outcomes. Certainly, it is up to leaders of organizations to build cultures that recognize and accept both visible and invisible differences in people.

Sexual Identity and the Cost of Repression

More people than ever have become aware of the increasingly open lives of LGBTQ people. This is evident in marriage rights extended to same-sex couples and the controversies surrounding the choice of bathroom by transgender people. Individuals who present as genderfluid—one day more masculine, another day more feminine—are also evident in today's workforce. What is missing in many organizations is acceptance, understanding, and respect.

Without awareness of the rights and interests of LGBTQ employees, it is not surprising that their contributions to business success often do not receive the same recognition provided to workers in the dominant demographic. When the views of LGBTQ people are discounted, the value of their unique perspectives and ideas for the betterment of the business are squandered.

Small wonder that many LGBTQ people hide their uniqueness in the workplace. In 28 U.S. states, in fact, they confront serious consequences for openly stating their sexual identity. Companies in those states can legally fire an employee for being lesbian, bisexual or gay. In 30 states, they can legally fire someone who is transgender. Obviously, to remain employed, LGBTQ individuals must visibly conform to the status quo, which consumes a substantial amount of energy that saps their focus and productivity.

Hiding one's sexual identity takes an extremely significant psychological toll, according to the work of Robert-Paul Juster, Ph.D., a Researcher at Centre de recherche de l'Institut universitaire en santé mentale de Montréal. Robert has studied the psychological and biological effects of stigmatizing LGB people in several controlled research projects. Compared with heterosexuals, closeted LGB people who experience perceived discrimination have more mood and anxiety disorders, suicidal ideation and attempts, are more often cigarette smokers, and have higher levels of alcohol and drug use. These devastating outcomes are attributed to higher levels of cortisol (the stress hormone).

"We collected the saliva of LGB people who were out, closeted LGB people, and heterosexual people to measure and compare their levels of cortisol," Robert explains. "While there were no major differences in biology stress indicators among the subjects by sexual orientation, the determining factor for the differences in cortisol levels was whether or not the LGB participants were out to their families and friends." The findings underline the important role that self-acceptance and disclosure have on an LGB person's positive health and well-being.

To obtain a more comprehensive profile, Robert and his fellow researchers also collected 20 physiological measures; including cholesterol, blood pressure, and glucose. Again, LGB people who were less avoidant about their 'coming out' had better health indicators. "Being out had a healthy, cathartic effect," Robert says.

"Our results from Montreal are in stark contrast to an initial study of another group in Arizona, a state with few LGBT protections. Here, gay and bisexual men who came out, specifically at work, had higher levels of cortisol—just the opposite effect. They also self-reported more negative emotional states than those who were not out at work." Where you live is also important in determining the health and wellness benefits of disclosure.

A 2016 study by L. Zachary DuBois starkly outlined the psychological impact of transitioning stressors among transgender men. Transgender men who experienced heightened stigma and stress related to their transitioning identity "coming out," and using public restrooms showed markedly-higher cortisol levels throughout the day compared to transgender men experiencing less social stress. "These findings among transgender men from Massachusetts and Vermont again show how stigma can 'get under the skin and skull' of marginalized people," says Robert, the senior author of this study. The researchers concluded that the discrimination that greeted these employees daily increased their stress levels.

Such discrimination is evident in the lower incomes that LGBTQ employees receive when compared to the incomes of heterosexual employees. A 2012 study by The Williams Institute, for example, reveals that gay and bisexual men earn 10 to 32 percent less than similarly qualified heterosexual men.

These varied experiences clearly show that much work

remains to bring resonance to workplaces. The experiences of people like Susan, John, Jarik and Deb, as well as the LGBTQ individuals in Robert's studies, are valuable in demonstrating how difference is a strength in a business context.

The issue is not people's surface differences, but how their unique experiences, personalities, and outlooks can contribute to everyone's greater well-being in the collective pursuit of business success. "The more people recognize that we are vastly more complementary than we are different, the less we will fear our differences," says Robert. "The hope is that we will actually celebrate them—to the benefit of everyone's health.

CHAPTER 4: GIGS, LATERALS AND STRETCH ASSIGNMENTS

The Nature of Work is Changing

People are switching jobs more frequently today than in preceding generations—in fact, for millennials, three times more than in previous generations (Gallup). This dynamic is attributed to both organizations and people. Organizations rarely give workers the variety of diverse assignments they may wish for to develop new skills and stay energized at work.

They often value job fitness over cultural belonging, whereby "fitting in" requires conscious effort on the part of individuals. For an organization to be in resonance with its workforce, it is increasingly important to rethink work structures and definitions, prioritizing people's pursuit of variety and new experiences in the company and a more fluid definition of the work they perform.

Old Workforce Structures No Longer Work

Organizations that maintain decades-old operating structures in an era of profound business, technological, and social changes are at significant competitive risk. Thanks to HR digitization and mobile and distributed technologies, business is conducted in real time. Layers of management and delegation of authority that slow down the speed of business are being altered. Many companies have had to accept that the physical location of the workplace can be anywhere. Beyond that, entire systems of production, the nature of management, and the ground rules and norms of governance are transforming rapidly across diverse industry sectors.

Here we can see some parallels with public education, a system first developed to prepare factory workers for assembly-line work. Today, very few people want jobs that involve repetitive manual tasks. Consequently, educational institutions are being disrupted because the status quo curriculums and methods of teaching no longer prepare people for the flexible, 24/7 mobile work environment. The emerging workforce requires new systems, processes, and means of performing work.

This disruption mirrors the struggles of many organizations when it comes to job fluidity. Workplaces are out of sync with how people can—and should—work. We know that technologies like social media, artificial intelligence (AI), mobile devices, interactive intranets, and the cloud unleash extraordinary possibilities for people to work better. As teamwork replaces the former "command and control" workforce structures, new work paradigms are emerging that involve more fluid notions of work, jobs, and the people who perform them.

I call this transformation *workforce fluidity*, which brings together *organizational fluidity* (the reality of how work gets done, alternative collaborative constructs, the absence of formal organization structures, and even team-based hiring) with *job fluidity* (people who are not identified by a specific job description but who flow between initiatives and supervisors, pursuing work that engages their curiosity and competence and fulfills organizational needs). After all, according the World Economic Forum, it is jobs—not people—that will become redundant in the future of work.

The Dynamic Organization: Workforce Fluidity

Workforce fluidity is emerging in parallel with the increasing importance and open dialogue about identity fluidity occurring across the globe. As individuals become more fluid in their identities, the lines between "profession," "career", and the "nature of work" are blurring. This fluidity encompasses not just flexible/virtual work assignments and collaborative teamwork, but also shifting corporate hierarchies. In some cases, it involves the elimination of job titles and even the construct of a job, replacing these norms by valuing the contributions of multiple teams and collective results instead.

These issues are not new in and of themselves. What is different is their convergence in the modern workplace. The interaction of these forces—identity fluidity, job fluidity, and organizational fluidity—is a powerful phenomenon.

These elements of fluidity cannot be understood in isolation, because each is a part of true workforce fluidity. Organizations that fail to thoughtfully address workforce fluidity in all its forms may run the risk of becoming less appealing work environments for employees and job seekers alike.

The Gig Economy

Today's businesses exist in the context of the global economy. They rely on a global workforce undergoing a fundamental transformation that challenges our notions of the nature and balance of traditional full-time work. The "gig economy" is a case in point.

People no longer have to hold full-time salaried jobs to earn an income. Contingent workers make up more than 40 percent of today's workforce. According to the U.S. Federal Government Accountability Office, this population includes independent contractors who provide a service or product, part-time workers, self-employed workers, contract company workers, agency temps, and on-call workers who cycle in and out of companies filling skillset voids on an as-needed basis.

Many companies value the financial benefits of employing gig workers. According to an analysis conducted by Joseph G. Hadzima Jr. for MIT Sloan School of Management, the total cost of a traditional employee can be as much as 1.4 times a person's base salary. For instance, the employer is not required to make contributions to Social Security, unemployment insurance and workers compensation, or manage tax withholding. Businesses also save on healthcare, sick leave, overtime and paid vacation time, and typically do not have to provide benefits like dental plans, life insurance, disability insurance, and even gym memberships—perks that highly-skilled full-time workers generally expect.

There is another equally powerful reason why the ranks of contingent workers are swelling—many people are fed up with traditional jobs that undervalue their talents, provide little to no opportunity to expand their skillsets, and do not consider their individuality and preferences. People are taking charge of their work lives, with employers forced to manage the turnover impact on an organization and its culture.

This has not been an easy task. According to the Randstadt "Workplace 2025" study, companies will begin to rely more heavily on an on-demand, agile workforce to remain competitive. More than 91 percent of employers agree that by 2025, employers will need to be more effective at workplace collaboration to manage a growing remote or virtual workforce.

Added to these growing differences in what constitutes an "employee" is the sheer age diversity of people in many businesses. For the first time in history, five different generations are members of the American workforce. Their aggregate expectations are vastly different, adding complexity to defining what work is and how it is conducted. The extraordinary speed of changes in the nature of work and the composition of today's workforce is outpacing many organizations' ability to make sense of it, much less harness these changes to inspire people in their shared pursuit of success.

As more companies employ a greater volume of non-salaried workers, HR must build a culture of innovation, collaboration, and empowerment that crosses over all the traditional areas it is responsible for—including recruiting, compensation and more.

It's a large responsibility, requiring significant investments of time and energy to understand and harness needed changes. But the rewards for businesses that take these steps are substantial. The disparate elements of the total workforce can be integrated into a cohesive unit of productive people inspired by the organization's purpose, culture, and values.

To attain this state, the best HR departments are developing total workforce strategies that leverage a single technology platform that provides visibility into all types of people. In doing so, HR improves their company's access to quality contingent hires, coordinating recruitment activities to employ the best types of workers to achieve business goals. Other benefits include faster onboarding, increased transparency for contract worker labor expenses, and enhanced corporate compliance with local and national employment laws and tax regulations.

"By having greater visibility into the blended workforce, companies can optimize talent to meet demand fluctuations, and balance labor costs with workforce agility," says Beth Roekle, president of Advantage xPO (U.S.), a provider of contingent and permanent workforce staffing solutions.

Roekle's clients tell her today's workforce is one in which many people are not aligned with the value of full-time employment as they were in the past. "They're much more likely to adopt a 'gig economy' outlook to their careers, even if they are being paid as a (full-time) employee," she says.

Does this evolving employee mindset affect feelings of company loyalty, causing distress for corporate leaders? In an October 2016 commissioned study conducted by Forrester Consulting on behalf of Ultimate Software, many answers emerged. Fifty percent of survey respondents—all HR leaders—stated that employees who change jobs frequently are a liability. Such "job hopping" is perceived as a red flag in the talent acquisition process. It is no wonder that many HR leaders are so protective of talent, taking steps to ensure people remain on their teams as long as possible.

Their concerns are understandable—talent acquisition is a constant process and can be a grind, hence they may shy away from hiring someone they perceive as a flight risk. HR leaders have an emotional reaction to potential employee turnover, and feel they must do all they can to avoid losing people with key skillsets and institutional knowledge. Yet, the reality is that at some point, HR leaders and organizations that don't adapt to the changes in the workforce will "lose" skilled and motivated employees, simply because their attention, energy and work behaviors will wane.

Now that the expectations of employment involve shorter timeframes, employee loyalty is no longer a given. Yet, loyalty can still exist—if it is construed in terms of loyalty to individual people, rather than the organization as a whole. It's reasonable to expect employee loyalty, but leaders need to start measuring it in terms of commitment, not length of employment. In this regard, the conversation about employee retention needs to change from "What can we do to keep them?" to "How can we help employees do their best work while they're with us?"

If you're an HR leader, you must help business leaders understand that no matter what you do, employees most likely won't work for the organization forever. At some point, they will likely pack up and leave for opportunities outside the company, if only to learn a different way of operating in another organization. It's up to you as a leader to accept this reality and make it work for your teams.

While these trends are beginning to reshape how companies operate and how people work, an even more profound shift is underway that will have a lasting effect on the workforce of the future—job fluidity.

Job Fluidity: The Nature of Work Expectations is Changing

Job fluidity exists today across all businesses, including more traditionally-structured organizations. People who prefer not to be tied to or identified by a specific job description are drawn to work opportunities where they can apply their curiosity, passion, and experience. They seek work that flows between initiatives and supervisors to maximize the breadth of their many talents. In this multi-skilled, multi-task setting, titles and job roles seem almost superfluous.

Let's face it, the moment a job description is completed, the work's nature and expectations change. Yet many companies still invest in exhaustive job description overhaul projects and continuously rework organization charts. Shoehorning modern workforce realities into an inflexible hierarchy will only result in a poor fit. While job descriptions have a place in recruitment and in communicating the general expectations for a position, jobs should be more open, allowing for expansion and extension.

With job fluidity, each employee becomes much more than the person's profession, title, or job description. Giving a worker the fluidity to move between multiple projects, tasks, or even job roles—without the restrictions imposed by formal transfers—presents an opportunity to explore personally-enriching experiences that also benefit the organization, as it results in more engaged, broadly talented and productive employees.

Job fluidity is comparable to identity fluidity—describing how employees self-identify, jettisoning binary descriptions like "he" or "she," and "introvert" or "extrovert." It is also analogous to organizational fluidity, where the reality of how work actually gets done has little to do with formal organization structures that confine a person's breadth of talents, and more with their ability to effectively collaborate with others.

These various movements in fluidity describe a new type of organization, one in which management is dynamically distributed across teams of people, rather than restricted to a hierarchical "command and control" structure. Categorizing an employee's job with a specific description and title is perceived as reductive, as it overlooks the many other talents that people possess and can contribute to the organization, in addition to their curiosity to learn new skills.

There is a humanistic element to this new organization, one that actually harks back to the beginnings of companies. The origin of the word "company" derives from the Latin word for "companion." Clearly, a "command and control" structure has very little to do with people companionably working together on a project or other initiative. A companion is someone with whom you can freely express (and comfortably receive) an opinion. In a work setting, colleagues should not be limited in the range of their ideas merely because of restrictive job descriptions.

If an employee's capabilities are not recognized and stretched, it increases their feelings of estrangement and disengagement from their work, culminating in unproductive behaviors and ultimately in retention problems for employers. Millennials, in particular, are especially prone to leaving an organization that limits the fullest expression of their ideas, or fails to fulfill their personal and career aspirations.

People want to be recruited by companies with a mission that is clear, purposeful, and meaningful, and then be given the autonomy to fulfill this mission the best they can. What they don't want are tightly-defined job descriptions that limit their capacity to learn and grow; or worse, that provide an "out," enabling people to avoid challenging themselves and being challenged by others "because it isn't part of the job." Give them a specific job title and a restricted set of responsibilities and they will learn all they can, then fly off to another company to acquire their next set of skills.

Employers cannot empower this new workforce without advocating fluid job assignments. Such assignments should be defined according to the work that needs to be accomplished, as opposed to an individual's perceived role in the organization. Jenny may be a terrific writer in the marketing department, who, by the way, also happens to be an excellent public speaker. What a waste of talent to keep her at a keyboard all day.

Although it may not be practical for all industries and people, by providing some level of experimentation with fluid job duties and assignment rotation (going well beyond low-risk internship programs), HR can encourage and enable unexpected collaborations and innovations to the benefit of all. Not all companies will reach full workforce fluidity, and not every organization will find optimal value from it. Still, it is a worthy initiative to contemplate, one that clearly affects workforce behaviors to produce value for customers, partners, colleagues, and other stakeholders.

CHAPTER 5: BEYOND AUTOMATION

Technology Alters Workflow, Not the Workforce

Technology has long been a powerful driver of changing people's expectations and behaviors inside and outside of work, and we are at the cusp of even more dramatic changes on the horizon. Therefore, no examination of workplaces and the workforce being out of sync is possible without exploring the impact of technology; from social platforms to artificial intelligence, process automation to distributed cognitive computing. In many organizations, technology has altered workflows but not the workplace experience in equal measure.

The challenge is one of proximity and inevitability. Even the most dedicated business and people leaders, HR professionals, and individual champions for resonance can't be everywhere at once to identify each nuanced change in their people. The good news is that new technologies are emerging that will be able to take up this human slack, when used appropriately. The second part of the challenge is that technological disruption and the exponential pace of technology change are inevitable, and missed opportunities to leverage technological advancements abound. HR technology is a case in point. The evolution of HR technology—from systems of record to systems of interaction—continue to be based on the same transactional foundations that are decades old. Technology, applied judiciously, could become a force multiplier in the move towards resonance. For now, this possibility remains elusive.

Technology: Not as Transformative as You Might Think...Yet

To understand how technology can play a role in addressing a lack of resonance between the workforce and the organization, we need to look at the evolution of technology inside companies. For centuries, people and the organizations they serve have used new forms of technology to do work more efficiently, cost-effectively and productively. With each technological revolution, new job and work opportunities have also arisen – because as is always the case with technology, change is constant.

The First Industrial Revolution, in the 18th and 19th centuries, introduced the use of water and steam power to mechanize production. The power loom, for example, transformed the English textile market by increasing volume and speed of production. Large-scale businesses became possible, and led to wide distribution to absorb added transport costs through greater sales, and moving sales out of local areas. Mechanized production affected every part of the process, changing where significant numbers of people lived and how they made a living. These new urban workplaces were often hazardous, and workers were exploited, especially women and children who were paid less than men for the same work.

The Second Industrial Revolution, from the late 19th to mid 20th century, used electric power to create mass production, fostering a worldwide industrial culture. The automobile assembly line replaced teams of workers who manufactured cars one at a time. Mass production brought down the cost of automobiles, opening up new markets beyond wealthy customers who could afford the original hand-made cars. A huge blue-collar working class emerged at this time and with it, a new kind of "specialization-focused" worker, which unfortunately resulted in less individual creativity and autonomy for people at work.

The Third Industrial Revolution, from the mid-20th through the beginnings of the 21st century, allowed hardware and software to automate production across global supply chains. Global communication between producers of raw materials and manufacturers became easier, and "just-in-time" manufacturing processes aligned with customer demand. The shift in the nature of jobs brought on by computers impacted women disproportionately, and tasks such as filing and manual computing were replaced by technology.

Now a Fourth Industrial Revolution—with AI as its central enabler—has arrived, characterized by a fusion of technologies blurring lines between the physical, digital, and biological. The Internet has removed physical and time barriers, and real-time peer-to-peer conversations happen across the globe. This results in incredible learning, commercial opportunities, and collaboration. Mobile and distributed devices let us communicate anywhere and at any time; and continued advances in robotics, machine learning, and smart machines are driving new business models and modes of human and machine interaction never before seen. The connection of many sources of rich data is available to more than 50 percent of the world's population in the cloud via the Internet and the Internet of things (IoT), but that means 50 percent of the population is still missing out on potential benefits.

These significant and extraordinary enhancements in communications and collaboration have changed the world of business, but they have not changed the fundamental practices, interactions, and experiences in the workplace, with the exception of remote work arrangements. Through several industrial revolutions, each one has involved innovative improvements in tools and processes to perform work efficiently and cost-effectively. Little, if any, focus has been placed on the lives of people using these technologies. Even today, minimal thought is given to the impact of digital transformation on the workforce—how technology can help a person thrive as an individual. For instance, does the IoT relate to people at work? Could it lead to the *Internet of People* at work?

Hopefully this paradigm is beginning to give way. There are significant differences between the first three revolutions and the current one. According to the World Economic Forum, today's industrial transformation is not merely a prolongation of the Third Industrial Revolution; it is distinct because of its velocity, scope and systems impact. The speed of current technological breakthroughs—and their corresponding impact on people's work lives—has no historical precedent. When compared with previous industrial revolutions, the Fourth represents an exponential rate of change, not a linear one, disrupting almost every industry in every country. The breadth and depth of these changes point to a transformation of entire business models, systems of production, management, and governance.

The State of Artificial Intelligence

A prime example of the need for a new mode of governance is the current global landscape of AI. The state of AI development is fragmented, and will require increased levels of cross-cultural collaboration to ensure it does not create and perpetuate dangerous biases that may reduce its many benefits for people and businesses. In 2017, Professor Vicente Ordóñez and colleagues at the University of Virginia found that AI systems that were trained on prominent research-image collections did not simply reflect the gender biases already present in those collections, but amplified them. The resulting gender bias associating women with kitchens was so strong the AI misclassified a man in a kitchen as a woman. We must do better, and that requires we look honestly at the global data that teaches AI and what course-corrections will be required to unite the divide to the benefit of people worldwide.

Technology outlets characterize the state of AI as an "arms race" between today's superpowers (the U.S. and China) and the "middle powers," what the *Bulletin of Atomic Scientists* called "countries like Australia, France, Singapore, and South Korea", among others. Because these "middle powers" typically have "more capital than labor" in comparison to the U.S. and China, their approach to AI is less about dominating the landscape than it is about shaping it and regulating its growth. For example, the British House of Lords advocated for UK-based companies to specialize in a narrower subset of artificial intelligence research, such as ethics or DE&I, instead of aiming to lead the market in every branch of the field.

In the shifting landscape of AI research and development, private companies—from startups to multinational giants—are rushing to take advantage of public funds and AI-friendly business "ecosystems" and leveraging those assets to position themselves and their home countries as players in the ongoing 'digital race'. While the U.S. and China still lead the pack in terms of the sheer number of AI-centric startups and development programs, just under a quarter of the organizations highlighted in CB Insights' "AI 100" Report are based out of "middle powers" that already play major roles in the tech industry as a whole, such as Japan, Israel, and Germany.

In the midst of this nationalist frenzy, we need a unifying strategy that considers the impact of AI on people more prominently. Ganesh Bell argued in a 2018 World Economic Forum article that the rush to capitalize on today's superpower rivalry will have to transform itself into a movement centered on collaboration. While China, the European Union, and India have taken steps to foster international cooperation and develop across-the board regulations for AI technologies, these efforts are incomplete and national advancement remains the most important motive for most countries' AI strategies. Reconciling this difference in attitudes will be crucial for delivering multicultural AI-based tools and systems that best serve people.

Technology in Support of the Changing Workforce

How can technology that uses AI ethically and is developed at the service of people support the changes needed to achieve resonance? For one thing, automating repetitive tasks—robotic processing automation (RPA)—can free people to pursue more challenging and strategic thinking and virtual reality can be used in recruiting to provide job seekers with immersive experiences. Imagine the power of interactive tools that allow a person to experience how a new job might "look and feel," or sentiment analysis tools that can help HR leaders pick up on the emotions and implicit biases that exist in the words people use. This kind of language analysis could help an organization address potential team challenges before they become damaging to an organization's resonance with its workforce.

Less than five years ago, virtual reality (VR) experiences were prohibitively expensive for organizations other than gaming companies, which could commercialize the experiences on a big scale. Today, creating a VR experience is not only affordable for more organizations (school districts have started using virtual reality to help elementary school children explore different careers), but it is also an excellent way to connect with tech-savvy candidates who want to be certain they are joining an organization that values technology.

Other promising applications of virtual reality in the workplace include kinesthetic employee development and job training where being physically on the job is too dangerous for novices. Even more experimental is VR's use to increase a person's empathy for others. By providing virtually shared experiences among different types of people, a more inclusive workplace environment can be attained. Imagine how impactful it would be to have someone who has never been a member of an underrepresented group experience a team meeting in which they are the only person of a certain race or sexual orientation in a "virtual" room. The VR Laboratory at Stanford University has documented this success in its experiments, giving people the virtual experience of a day in the life of a refugee, to create empathy for displaced migrant populations. The possibilities are endless and incredibly exciting.

Cognitive Computing, Human-Machine Interfaces, and Ambient HR

A variety of "people-first/people-centered" inter-connected technologies augmenting global workforce capabilities is taking root in the HR landscape. These tools embrace cognitive computing—the simulation of human thought processes in a computerized model. Typically, these solutions are lumped together as AI, a term that has been around for decades but continues to elude precise definition. Often, AI evokes nefarious job-stealing robots, if not quite the Terminator or the robot HAL from *2001: A Space Odyssey*. Some people believe insights drawn from AI are somehow "artificial" or less than true.

A more apt and less stress-invoking definition of AI is that of a tool that mimics but does not replace human cognitive processes. In other words, AI augments human capabilities by processing enormous volumes of data at great speed, unburdening human beings in this work.

Any time a new technology is introduced, there are labor implications. The difference now is the risk, breadth, and scope of job displacement and wide-scale awareness of its imminence—even if they occur many years in the future.

Businesses maintain that their investments in cognitive computing will free up people to provide them with more interesting value-added work. A case in point is finance, where RPA is being widely deployed to perform account reconciliations and journal entries. Rather than crunch the numbers, accountants are now free to make sense of them for strategic decision-making purposes, a very real benefit for their teams, provided the organization understands what motivates the impacted individuals.

Today we can easily imagine a future in which robotics are ubiquitous in the workplace and what that will mean for employee experiences across the globe. Yet organizations have new opportunities, using AI, to improve the quality of human interactions. AI can conceivably power a new era of "Ambient HR" that could augment HR professionals' ability to listen to the voice of employees (VoE) with greater understanding and comprehension. It can further allow HR to "be" in more than one place at a time, gathering the sentiments of employees through distributed data-collection interfaces that capture human communication and emotion.

These new aggregations of cognitive-capable distributed technology will finally transform HR's impact on the business from providing summaries of transaction-focused tactical insights that rely on people to selectively provide feedback into a "smart" human ecosystem.

Voice-interface interactions and smart sentiment-analysis solutions are arising in part as a response to the traditionally slimmed-down capabilities of self-service solutions. Such systems forced employees and managers to "serve themselves" from a limited set of actions and information deemed appropriate for casual technology users. Employees who are used to using Digit or other financial saving apps would find a payroll summary in employee self-service to be archaic and of little value. The prevalence of technology in everyone's life makes these limitations increasingly inappropriate.

A new generation of "smart" or perceptive tools able to derive sentiment from simple text and action patterns not only allows users to quickly engage with leadership by sharing their perspectives about a new benefit policy rollout or reorganization, but also gives leaders an immediate analysis of employee emotions and cultural themes with regard to the success of the new investment.

Taken in the context of daily work, richly human insights derived from interaction data are critical to serving people with technology. Not only do they provide ongoing interaction patterns that can tailor experiences for employees, but HR leaders can use them to proactively provide reminders to global employees with meaningful and personalized context, encourage them to take actions that advance their work, and inspire their team members.

The HR Connection

Automation is at the root of all business software. HR software, for instance, was created first to collect and store "personnel" data, then to avoid payroll calculation errors, and soon after, to automate multi-step, often paper-intensive traditional HR processes like performance evaluations and benefits enrollment.

Because HR systems were historically designed to store data and automate processes, there is concern that more sophisticated HR software powered by AI will "automate away" HR jobs. Part of this fear stems from the fact that HR departments have traditionally been classified as cost centers, not value creation centers; as a result, there is a history of attempts to outsource the HR function entirely.

These experiments have not mostly not succeeded, but have left HR uneasy. For example, after a company adopts HR payroll software, the payroll staff may worry their department will be downsized or eliminated because the automated system is more efficient. However, efficiency, as we discussed in the example above of robotic process automation (RPA), also frees people up to do other things. In the case of payroll professionals, automation can liberate them from mundane tasks to focus on proactively solving the most complex errors, and the more thoughtful work of ensuring payroll programs are having the intended positive business outcomes, or that people are able to better manage their financial wellness with new insights into their pay.

Niche and best-of-breed software providers have multiplied in the last 20 years, with offerings designed to improve recruiting, onboarding, talent development (primarily learning and career "pathing"), and survey and engagement tools to assess employees' feelings about their jobs and work. These tools have yet to be fully effective, since the larger systems in which they are embedded have not fundamentally altered. Until technology providers can shift from transactional tracking systems to experiential people-centered systems of interaction, organizations will struggle to get broad adoption of their technology investments.

Today's workers want their leaders and organizations to hear their concerns, to be open to more communication in the context of their work, and to provide greater purpose and meaning to this work. Smart technologies—such as cognitive computing and distributed technology extending beyond mobile in the cloud—have unleashed extraordinary possibilities for people at work.

We now have the opportunity to do much more than just automate processes to increase efficiency; we can now begin to better understand people, the driving force at the core of the HR profession. In the past, we tossed more work at people without necessarily understanding the emotional toll of these added responsibilities. When used thoughtfully, HR technology gives us the chance to create compelling experiences, parse just how employees feel about their work and their work lives at scale, and know what motivates them (or doesn't).

When I say "at scale," I mean that technology can augment traditional conversations. With today's geographically dispersed workforce, it's now possible after every work activity to ask someone how things went, how they felt about it, and if they feel successful and fulfilled. If we deploy new technologies such as Natural Language Processing (NLP) not just to automate, but also to understand people and interpret the meaning behind what people say, we have the opportunity to truly go beyond automation to something vastly different.

With the help of these new technologies, we can begin the complex work of comprehending people more completely and defining solutions that help them succeed, however they choose to define success. We will know when something happens in the workplace that tragically demotivates them or energizes them. Technologies that are designed to perceive deeply will give people leaders a critical source of information to process their employees' sentiments in real time. This data can drive more meaningful and informed conversations with employees to better understand their work experience and how to improve it for the good of all parties. The tools also can help leaders prepare for the emotional responses to an organizational change.

For resonance to become a reality, businesses need to widely adopt these new experiential technologies and make them the foundation of their people-centered HR technology system. The technologies have immense potential to create highly personalized digital employee experiences and significant differentiation and competitive advantage in the future of work. Rather than just knowing how long an employee took to complete a required online course (a transactional interpretation of data), wouldn't it be more valuable to know how they felt while they were learning, if they were engaged and retained the knowledge? At the end of the day, the most valuable new technologies must be about making people better and smarter.

Technology For the People

Nearly half the workforce today is composed of individuals who grew up steeped in technology at home and at school, with textbooks replaced by tablets. These digital natives are not only adept at using technology, but are also dependent on it in their routine interactions. Businesses that understand how people actually use technology will have a significant competitive edge. To seize this opportunity, they must deploy personalized solutions that meet the needs of employees and customers and can be easily configured for unforeseen change.

For example, a new vernacular has permeated popular culture and is making its way into the workplace. I'm referring to multiple gender designations, non-binary sex, and self-defined ethnicity. Systems must be able to support the use of these new terms, elevating system configurability as an absolute must for modern organizations. Companies need to accommodate new definitions of how employees identify themselves, or risk the negative impacts of people not being able to be as much themselves at work as they are in their lives outside of work.

Technology that facilitates configuration on the fly, remote collaboration, and temporary team creation for short-term problem-solving becomes a work imperative beyond simply tagging an individual's work-group affiliations for identification.

Finally, because non-traditional workers currently make up 20 to 30 percent of the workforce, and by 2020 50 percent of the Canadian and American workforce will include five generations, and part- or full-time freelancers. Technology must be able to accommodate flexible and virtual work schedules that fill short-term assignments—a necessity in a global world of work with 24/7 connectivity. Consequently, organizations will need new and more extensible systems that both engage people and address rapidly changing work models.

HR must take charge in reinventing the technology behind the workforce so it serves people. This is an enormous responsibility, ensuring current and future technology takes into account the need to improve every employee's experience and success. Tools should be an extension of the individual, not just another technology distraction or information tracking system.

I'm optimistic we will move beyond automation to provide people with technology that understands human emotions and drivers at work, leveraging this insight to augment and amplify what people can achieve.

The Technology of Collaboration in Practice

Jeremy Scrivens is Managing Director of The Emotional Economy at Work, at the University of Western Australia's St. Georges College, and focuses on the emotional qualities of people in their work. "The problem with work today," he told me, "is that people who have been the operators of processes since the Industrial Age are suddenly dispensable. If people are going to be displaced to some extent by robots in future, why they need to work at all must be reappraised."

Cognitive computing technology, Jeremy believes, is not just a way to free people from being gears in a machine; it is also an opportunity for companies to liberate people to make deeper interpersonal connections that augment their ability to be more fully human at work. To reach this state, businesses must be open to new tools, but also consider their implications beyond just revenue and profits—providing meaningful and consequential responsibilities to people to make the world a better place.

In this regard, Jeremy advocates that companies replace their current organizational paradigms of hierarchically-structured work responsibilities with collaborative engagements in which everyone co-innovates a shared future. This is the work he does in his projects for companies and governments. In all cases, he creates a physical "appreciative inquiry summit" and a virtual "social room." Both approaches call for bringing together people in open discussions.

The concept recently was put to work on behalf of the town of Alloa, a flourishing port town in Scotland until the 1970s, when road and rail eliminated the need for ships. The town subsequently fell on hard times. Numerous government working parties tried and failed to ignite new business initiatives.

Jeremy was called in to help in 2017. He presided over an appreciative inquiry summit in which local townspeople and decision makers were asked to define what was truly special about Alloa. "I wanted to change the conversation from what was not working to what was possible," he explains. "I asked them to recall when they had felt most alive in the town and to share these stories in small groups. I wanted them to shift from hopelessness to possibility—to imagine their future story."

However, the participants had a tough time coming up with ideas—that's how hard the town had fallen. Ultimately, they decided that Alloa was the hugging capital of Scotland. Jeremy's next step was to guide them to further connect and collaborate with others toward spreading this message in the virtual social room—via #hugs.

Invigorated for the first time in decades, the townspeople coalesced around such collaborative endeavors as adorning local businesses with more Christmas lights over the holidays than any other small town in Scotland. Suddenly Alloa got media attention, which led to interest among private and public sector organizations to set up operations and do business there.

Other cities across Scotland have now reached out to Jeremy to create similar summits and social rooms. In the end, the people of Alloa were compelled by events beyond their control to reimagine their future.

CHAPTER 6: THE BELONGING IMPERATIVE

Why D,E & I(B) is Critical for Achieving Resonance

When I talked with HR leaders in 2016 about the wishes of younger entrants to the workforce, they would acknowledge, often in exasperation, that new hires were very comfortable saying what they want from their work, what their service was worth, and when they expect to be promoted. In a 2016 study by the Center for Generational Kinetics, for example, roughly one-fifth of employees born after 1996 (Generation Z) said they expect quarterly promotions.

Evidently, in their career paths and expectations, younger employees are great self-advocates. Consequently, HR leaders have come to recognize that their biggest challenges lie not with new workers, but with their most tenured employees, who do not adapt to the dynamic, ever-changing and technologically-fueled future of work.

Many seasoned employees (I'm one of them) would

have loved to have been able to express our career goals and expectations 20 to 30 years ago. But it was a different era and that simply wasn't done. Now, employees across the board are taking a cue from their new colleagues, seeking this more open approach as a replacement for more rigid job and work structures.

In this new environment, many organizations are investing significant resources in redefining engagement, leadership, and diversity and inclusion initiatives. They want to ensure the myriad expectations of our transformed workforce are not met with roadblocks, in the form of antiquated organizational structures and processes that impede the benefits of diverse thinking and approaches to work.

The New Workforce: Diversity

Today's workforce is made up of a broad range of previously underrepresented groups of people—women, people of color, immigrants, disabled people, and LGBTQ individuals. In the United States, the Civil Rights Act of 1964 provides legal protections for employment and disallows discrimination in job hiring, termination, and promotions based on a person's race, color, creed, and gender, but the legislation does not extend to a person's sexual orientation or transgender status.

In many parts of America, particularly large urban centers of business, companies hire people specifically for their diversity. However, in other parts of the country, workplaces poorly reflect the diversity in our culture. The reason given is that diverse talent is not readily available, which is an all-too-easy excuse.

For the most part, newer arrivals to the workforce are comfortable with diversity. They are accepting of and even expect diversity as a natural priority in their education and work institutions. But often our workplaces are full of biases that don't represent what is actually happening in the world around us, and that needs to change for people to be in resonance with our organizations.

D&I initiatives and programs have entered the mainstream and moved beyond the realm of HR. In fact, D&I is increasingly becoming a component of companies' employee recruitment and customer branding strategies. Businesses promote their D&I statistics to candidates in online recruiting materials and solutions and in annual report images, noting percentages of employed women, African Americans, Hispanics, LGBTQ, disabled, and other underrepresented employee groups. Microsoft now publishes a comprehensive workforce demographic report as one measure of its progress toward a more diverse and inclusive Microsoft, and its contribution to the diversity of the tech industry overall. The message is that the business values the contributions of all people, no matter their differences. Organizations that do not provide this information must answer to candidates factoring workforce diversity into their employment decisions. Progress has been made.

The problem is that these messages, images, and statistics focus on apparent diversity, which is fairly easy to manufacture in photographs and almost as easy to create and tally up with targeted hiring practices. Yet the truth about diversity is more nuanced. Both visible and unseen differences exist. Consequently, hiring for diversity does not ensure lasting diversity, resulting in a hidden “revolving door” of inequity in promotions, pay, and other critical measures of workplace health.

Adding to the complexity is that people may opt out of categorization. For example, an increasing number of employees are choosing to not identify as a single ethnic category, with more people stating that their heritage as “mixed.” Women may choose not to participate in programs designed to benefit women because they want to be judged solely on their merits and not their gender, often knowing that the playing field is anything but uniformly equal and that meritocracy is a myth.

From Diversity to Inclusion

Inclusion—the feeling of belonging that comes about when employees are treated equitably and are free to bring their authentic selves to work—is equally problematic. Despite gradual advancements brought about by laws and changing employment practices, more diverse workforces are not necessarily more inclusive.

Creating an authentic culture of inclusion is much harder than achieving workforce diversity, yet it is just as critical. Without inclusion, if people sense that others judge them because they are “different,” this may adversely affect their self-esteem, freedom of expression, ability to collaborate openly, and their overall work engagement and productivity.

Why do so many companies fail at inclusion? One answer is implicit bias—ingrained stereotypes about different people that cloud the thinking of the dominant cultural paradigm, affecting understanding and decision-making. Implicit bias is not all-out racism, sexism, or any of the other –isms. All people are susceptible to snap judgments with no basis in fact about perceived differences—it's hard-wired into our DNA. We do our best to ignore these instincts, but they're frustratingly resilient, coloring our decisions and perceptions in ways we may not even realize.

While outward signs of prejudice can be met with immediate reprimands or job termination, implicit bias (or unconscious bias, as it is also called) is more difficult to perceive and manage. Unfortunately, this more subtle form of prejudice is pervasive and enduring in all businesses. According to a report by the National Institutes of Health, many people who outwardly profess no prejudice inwardly demonstrate bias. Researchers in the report uncovered evidence of unconscious racial bias by using Magnetic Resonance Imaging (MRI) brain scans. When shown pictures of people different than themselves, the study subjects' brains responded with alarm. Although they were not consciously aware of racist, sexist, or homophobic feelings, their unconscious racism, sexism, and homophobia was measurable. Why this appears to be the case is unknown, although the studies suggest that it may stem from humans' fight or flight response to a danger.

Other studies affirm that implicit bias is widespread. Again drawing on information from MRI scans, these reports indicate people tend to feel less empathy for others who appear different than they are, while feeling more empathy for individuals who appear the same. Expressed in human terms, a white, straight woman who reads about the plight of an African-American woman, a straight or gay man, or someone from a different cultural background feels less empathy for their duress than when reading about the plight of another white, straight woman.

Whereas diversity can be measured across types of people, inclusion has to do with each person's feelings about how the dominant or standard of workers in the organization perceive them. My point is that eradicating implicit biases to make all employees feel valued, respected, and supported is far more difficult—yet more important—than tallying up varied demographic metrics. It will not be easy to value the contributions of underrepresented people equally with those of the majority without significantly changing our thinking about team dynamics and who we hold responsible for inclusion. Yet this effort is certainly worth it, as inclusion is the key to unlocking the business benefits available from the unique ideas, perspectives and experiences of diverse people.

To seize this value, a team's culture must adapt to include the cultures of all people in the group. A woman joining an all-male team, for example, often feels like she must conform to the team's values and behaviors, or worse, is told by her manager that she is responsible for making others feel comfortable with her as the outlier. This changes her desire to express her ideas and opinions, reducing the possibility of success for the overall group dynamic. A better scenario would be for the men on the team to incorporate the values and behaviors of the woman into its culture.

This same approach applies to people of color, a different religion, sexual orientation, and so on. For diverse ideas, perspectives and opinions to flourish, the culture of the company and its leadership must transform. This transformation must be continuous and dynamic, incorporating and valuing the uniqueness that wide-ranging differences bring to a team.

Having a woman or a person of color or those with different abilities on a team automatically changes the team's culture, not the other way around. Companies are just beginning to recognize what this means—Google and Ultimate Software designate parking spots for women who are pregnant, and Accenture, IBM and Twitter send nursing milk overnight to dads at home to feed their infants while moms are away on business.

Inclusion is based on bringing all people together as a whole, and belonging (a term growing in popularity) goes further, to imply that no force or governing body is needed to include others to create a unified group of people. Most importantly, inclusion and belonging are not about numbers, a snapshot of counts in time, or fitting in, which requires effort. Rather, inclusion and belonging requires an ongoing series of concerted efforts to ensure diversity thrives and self-perpetuates and that underrepresented people are developed, paid, and promoted equitably.

A workforce of diverse individuals can show that a company is open to people's differences and has a commitment to creating a well-balanced team. Inclusion indicates the company welcomes their ideas, perspectives, and opinions, and belonging signals that their thoughts and contributions are inherently valued.

Tremendous business opportunities are available to companies that value the contributions of all their employees, whether they're gay or straight, black or white. The more extensive the diversity of people in an organization, the greater the possibility of generating unique ideas and innovating.

This is the longstanding view of Vivian (Viv) Maza, Chief People Officer at Ultimate Software, a provider of cloud-based human capital management solutions. Viv has been with the company since its inception in 1990, as it has grown from four people in four cubicles to more than 6,000 employees worldwide. While inclusion and belonging are common buzzwords today, Viv was practicing these words well before she was a part of Ultimate's founding team. She is quick to say that diversity and inclusion are two different things, yet many companies tend to lump them together, believing a diverse workforce is the same thing as an inclusive one. "Inclusivity is one of our core principles here," Viv says.

As the mother of two gay children, Viv has a personal connection to the need for all individuals, LGBTQ employees in particular, to be fully themselves at work as they are in life. "When someone comes out as gay, telling their parents or their employer, they're so nervous," she says. "I recall one employee who came out to me. I told him that being openly gay didn't change the dynamic of the special person he was. I wanted him to be as comfortable with himself as I was with him."

Viv pointed out that the company has many talented and gifted employees who are gay, but not all of them are "out." "The decision to come out, of course, is up to them, but I can promise them that this is a safe place of belonging for all our amazing people," she says. "We value each and every person's contributions, regardless of their differences. In fact, we cherish their differences."

Viv's feelings about inclusion extend to other aspects of personal self-identification. She recalled a job interview last year with a young woman who mentioned her previous employer had fired her because she had purple-colored hair. "I told her purple hair looks amazing and if that is how she defines herself, bring it on," says Viv. "Twenty years ago, we might have questioned her choice. But this is a new age, in which things that weren't acceptable at work are now seen as liberating. Work cultures used to be so conformist. Today they're dynamic, and that's a good thing."

I think of corporate culture not as a fixed set of standards, but as a living, breathing, and evolving entity. When a new person joins a team, the culture of the group changes and expands, enriched by the new person's experiences and perspectives. If the individual feels he or she has to conform to the dynamics of the team, the group suffers the loss of the person's unique viewpoint. The new employee might feel uncomfortable expressing a novel thought or a different opinion without fear of embarrassment, or worse, humiliation and eventual exclusion. Yet, all it takes is one extraordinary idea to upend the status quo.

So what exactly can an "optimal" culture look like? Viv imagines a future in which every employee feels their unique attributes and abilities are making a difference in a shared journey toward providing meaningful service. "Labels are worthless," says Viv. "What's crucial is to create an environment where people feel safe and supported being who they are."

How to Create Workplaces that are Resonant with Identity

A resonant workplace benefits organizational strength as much as it benefits the people working within it. When organizations are inclusive of the total workforce population, improved financial results, a stronger economy, and a better society result.

Since the starting line is always different for underrepresented groups, companies building resonant organizations may need to tip the scales in favor of women, people of color, LGBTQ individuals, and neurodiverse people to achieve balance and desired outcomes.

A culture that supports everyone in the workplace is a culture in which all people can flourish and achieve wonderful things.

While a resonant workplace makes managing and leading a workforce more complicated and challenging, it opens the door to new realms of economic opportunity. The incredible diversity of today's workforce encompasses cultural attributes that will help companies create, enrich, and deliver new products and services for the entire spectrum of the world's population. This opportunity contrasts with the development of products designed by one type of person with one mindset—an introverted white male software engineer, for example. With more diverse teams, businesses have an untapped opportunity to innovate and create truly game-changing products and services.

Those of us in the HR arena are bearing witness to these profound societal changes, perhaps more so than our colleagues in the rest of the organization. Certainly, this is disruptive, as are all sociocultural shifts. Inclusivity and belonging are at the crux of creating resonance between workplaces and the workforce. As people challenge the traditional classifications of their lives outside of work, they will increasingly expect their fellow employees across five generations to respect, understand and appreciate their individuality.

CHAPTER 7: MOVING TOWARDS RESONANCE

First, Know Where You are Starting

What's the best way to move towards resonance? First, understand the people in your organization—their readiness for change and diversity composition—to ensure your efforts will be representative and increase your chances for success. Then, examine the structure of your workplace to see how far it must evolve to become fluid, responsive, and open to a new mode of work. This process will position you to create a vision—an aspirational ideal of a vastly different future state that will guide how you reimagine your organization.

Deeply Understanding People

In recent years, employee engagement has been on every HR and business leader's mind. The value of having a highly engaged workforce for an organization's success is undeniable, but the way forward has remained elusive. To move towards resonance, you first need to know where you stand.

As much as 51 percent of the global workforce feels disengaged at work, according to Gallup, outnumbering actively engaged employees by a ratio of 2:1. These numbers have remained largely unchanged for 30 years, despite all the dialogue about employee engagement. Clearly, something is missing.

Engagement itself isn't the problem. Engagement is an outcome—a measure of overall employee experience and success, as defined by each person, which is far more nuanced and complex to understand. Engagement is about bringing out the best in people, earning their discretionary effort, and tapping into their full potential on a day-to-day basis. For this to happen, we must think of the employee experience in as much detail as we do the customer experience, which requires continual and honest assessment and communication.

Achieving an optimal employee experience demands a culture of openness and trust, and an environment in which people are not afraid to fail or approach leaders. This allows people to find purpose and meaning in their contributions. It also requires effective leaders who encourage employees to discover, unlock, and fulfill their potential in the workplace. The question then becomes twofold: What do we do to create an optimized employee experience, and how do we know when we've got it?

The answer is to create an atmosphere in which your employees feel free to voice their true thoughts and feelings about their work and the workplace, generating a culture that truly respects the "voice" of the employee. Once you genuinely listen to this voice and act on it, a transformation in employee experience is possible.

Employee voice is not the same as employee feedback, which often takes the form of traditional employee engagement surveys and newer pulse surveys. For employees voice to effectively emerge, each person must feel safe to share their honest opinions. The voice of the employee, in essence, reflects employees' actual experiences at work. Until people believe that you will listen to their truthful voice, employee engagement data may be skewed. People may self-edit their feedback, say what they believe you want them to say, or worse, remain silent.

Only when an organization has demonstrated through policy and action that everyone can be their true selves at work will they be open and honest. In this climate, efforts to hear the employee voice will result in an accurate appraisal of employee engagement. At that point, the employee experience can be optimized.

At a presentation for HR leaders, I once heard an audience member affirm the importance of listening to employees, recounting a recent exit interview with a valued employee. The employee told the interviewer that she would ask questions of her manager and never got a response. "I just wanted a response," she said. "I could have handled the answer either way, but I never (even) got a response."

We all get busy with day-to-day demands and might assume that not responding would be an indication that we're busy or don't yet have an answer. But the employee asking the question may feel the question asked didn't merit a response. Clearly, our assumptions can backfire, as this HR leader found out.

Who Exactly are Your People?

As we discussed earlier, people are comfortable identifying themselves in new ways. We also have seen the negative impact of not being able to be one's authentic self at work. If you are a business leader or an HR professional, the critical question is, do you really know who each person is versus how they present or pass at work? Might your employees be reluctant to be fully themselves? If this is the case, it connects back to the need to develop trust and safety in the work environment.

Certainly, at some point you'll need to know who they are and what their bigger picture is, to develop programs and initiatives that directly support them and create equity across the organization. Some information, such as available data on pay equity, is easy to find. A more complete picture of your workforce can be drawn by analyzing transactional data from business systems, employee surveys, and pulse feedback.

Start by answering basic questions about the workforce. Break down the data—percentages of men and women; ethnicity; age diversity; known gender diversity; and known neurodiversity—being aware that categorization itself can perpetuate biases. As you deepen your understanding of the workforce, you will discover missing information. Don't be surprised if there are large gaps—most organizations are in the same position.

Try to determine the composition of the organization as a whole, such as the composition of your leadership from team leader to the C-suite. Gathering this information is important if you want to move the workplace towards resonance. If you make no effort to understand the workforce more deeply than in the past, you will lack the information needed to make this journey.

Examining Structure

Next, take a look at the workplace structure. Does pay equity exist across different disciplines and functions? If not, are there areas where you are closer to this goal in some parts of your organization? Why not in others? Earlier, I discussed the need for organizations to accommodate job fluidity, fully integrate gig workers, and create possibilities for lateral moves and career pathing to pursue myriad work experiences.

It's not realistic to expect an organization to suddenly rebuild itself overnight. A great place to start is to identify areas of the business that are most adaptable or most in need of change. Perhaps the organization has natural operating cycles that require teams to staff up, such as year-end or seasonal peaks. Could employees from other areas of the organization shift focus to assist the overloaded teams, and in so doing gain valuable new skills and bring an innovative infusion of ideas to the busiest teams?

While audition-based flex projects and stretch assignments found on an internal talent marketplace (a repurposed internal opportunity job board) might seem farfetched, many organizations, from large restaurant chains to tech and media companies, have benefitted by implementing flex-team models with continuous learning opportunities for their employees. Many companies also provide the opportunity for employees to apply for programs that allow them to contribute to projects or become initiative leaders outside their current work group, resulting in an influx of fresh new perspectives about their work when they return to their former team and work.

The Role of HR in Creating Resonance

The key to beginning your transformation to a resonant workplace is to understand the new normal for employees, and to identify where to change work structures and configurations to reach the ideal point of resonance and amplification of productivity.

HR plays a crucial role in all of the above. Although other individuals in the organization are critical stakeholders, the day-to-day transformative work that creates resonance falls into the hands of HR professionals to define and initiate.

The HR profession is grounded in a history of industrial relations born of labor strife; personnel management designed to ensure compliance, work efficiency, and accurate tracking of labor; and more recently, the discipline of organizational behavior.

How is it that this human-centered profession is now accused of being a barrier to getting people hired and work done? Have HR leaders and departments lost sight of what is important, and what they must do to develop and empower the global workforce of the future? I say most definitely not.

When talking with HR professionals, they invariably describe how they joined the profession to serve people, to help employees attain their fullest potential, and to help shape the organization's culture to motivate and engage people (The Jensen Group, 2018). Yet, HR today is often faced with the internal perception that it serves the organization and not the people within it. This is particularly true in cases of sexual harassment and other employee grievances, as made clear by the #metoo movement and public outings of harassers at mega-enterprises like Nike and CBS.

Much of this disillusionment may stem from the internal discord and tension inherent in the modern role of the HR professional. HR's charter today is to create the best experience for the people in the employ of the organization. HR is tasked with empowering and developing employees, finding the best talent and retaining that talent in a positive work environment, alongside more traditional benefits and compensation administration. HR is expected both to do right by people in the organization and simultaneously help the organization carry out its objectives and fulfill its vision.

In this environment, HR teams and leaders need to turn the mirror on themselves. There is no doubt that too many traditional HR structures and processes are no longer relevant, yet HR and employees continue to be held by outdated expectations.

How should HR leaders evolve to achieve resonance? They must begin by making critical changes to traditional

HR norms and practices immediately, beginning with reflections on employee compensation, benefits, performance and recognition.

How Do We Compensate?

Compensation has traditionally been position- or job-based. Workers are rewarded for the kind of work they do, with geographic differentials where required. Little consideration is given an employee's stage in life or personal circumstances. This approach seems counterintuitive when you think about the vast differences in compensation requirements for a 20-year-old entrant into the workforce versus a veteran employee possibly caring for elderly family members or paying for their children's college tuition.

When I was starting out and had two young children, bonuses meant nothing to me—I wanted a predictable salary. I needed to know what to expect as my income, every paycheck. Variable compensation plans were not nearly as compelling to me then as they are today with a house nearly paid off and my children almost through college. I've saved for retirement. I'm more comfortable with having more of my compensation in stock or bonus-based.

Another relevant motivator governing how people want to be paid—along with compensation allocations like cash, restricted stock, bonus, and in-kind benefits—is personality (even more so than job type). Some individuals are extrinsically motivated; for example, a salesperson may want to "blow out" their sales goals. This motivation should be reflected by the compensation structure; it also should be rewarded, assuming the organizational culture celebrates such performance.

On the other hand, an intrinsically-motivated individual might not choose a financially-centered form of compensation. Instead, the person might request greater work responsibilities or a change in job title or status, with a commensurate increase in pay. Such people tend to prioritize respect for a job well done, and the recognition that goes along with it.

Most importantly, to provide employees a voice, compensation plans and payout approaches must be reinvented. That may mean offering on-demand pay options for employees who may not be able to wait until a set pay date to be paid for the work they've done. Compensation plans are designed to motivate people and reward them for behaviors that serve the organization, ideally resulting in the top performance of both people and the business.

However, if a compensation plan is based purely on the role that someone performs, it may not motivate the individual, impeding expected behaviors and business outcomes. By tailoring compensation to employees' needs, companies can reduce their financial stress and improve their quality of life, resulting in a better incented and successful workforce.

There may be merit in a lifecycle-based compensation plan, whereby employees have the opportunity to change their compensation structure over time to best meet their current needs. For example, HR or the organization might allow employees to reevaluate and readjust their compensation structure every three to five years, based on predetermined criteria. Broader and more inventive incentive-based compensation plans could also reward employee performance and results regardless of hours worked, providing more flexible work hours and paid-time-off programs.

Recognition

Employee recognition has always tended towards publicly acknowledging an employee's performance and contributions, often in the form of awards, ceremonies or leaderboards. While this approach may suit individuals who like public recognition, more introverted people may be mortified. The point is that resonant recognition is not a one-size-fits-all endeavor.

The most successful recognition programs are based on understanding the variances in employee preferences, motivations and values. For people who are extrinsically motivated, a competitive award and bonus makes perfect sense as a way to recognize these individuals. On the other hand, a more introverted employee might want an extra PTO day with family rather than public recognition, while yet another may prefer a bonus.

HR must get more creative in compensating and recognizing employees, considering their personality and current stage in life. At different points in their employment when networking and brand-building are critical, recognition could be in the form of a lunch with a higher-ranking executive to help propel their career. Rewards should be as unique as the individuals who receive them.

The possibilities are endless. The key is to train team leaders to personally recognize and appropriately extol the accomplishments of every person under their supervision. This approach requires a high degree of empathy and approachability to drive optimal organizational performance.

Performance

The traditional annual performance management process has been lambasted in recent years as demotivating for employees and antithetical to performance improvement. Studies have demonstrated the many drawbacks of forced ranking, annual reviews with performance scores, and pay for performance schemes from biased reviewers. Other minuses include wasteful time expenditures and stress-induced disengagement.

In response, many HR departments and business leaders are moving toward continuous employee feedback. This approach has tremendous merit. The emphasis is placed on a person's recent or forthcoming work, removing such barriers to top performance as scores for months-old accomplishments.

Unfortunately, most approaches to performance management have been centered on an individual's actions, behaviors, and accomplishments. In a resonant workplace, a person's impact on others must register as part of their performance. Other actions, such as how someone has contributed to a legacy of inclusion or inspired colleagues to be more productive, should similarly factor into their performance assessment and conversation. For example, if the leader of a software development team continually promotes women, people of color, and neurodiverse individuals to management positions, the person should be rewarded for the positive impact on the organization and the growth in the accomplishments and responsibilities of team members.

Such a leader is a force multiplier for the company, and not necessarily for themselves. As in a relay race, the first, second, and third baton carriers get less recognition than the finisher; yet, all team members must perform their best to achieve victory.

Shifting from evaluating employees' past performance to developing the future performance of people and teams should be another performance management objective. This approach requires the use of smart technologies to aggregate crowd sourced comments and correlate them with performance changes over time. If performance is to have meaning for both people and organizations we must expand the scope of performance from the achievements of an individual to the person's impact on team members and the entire organization.

HR Transformed: A New Way

The HR function is caught between a rock and a hard place—designed to be employee advocates but destined to be employer advocates by virtue of who pays their way. This antagonistic dynamic must be eased in such a way that the two "sides" of the problem actually support each other.

We have already described how new entrants to the workforce are more comfortable than previous generations in expressing their work demands and expectations. At the same time, employers facing labor shortages for certain skill sets are recognizing that their competitive advantage is people. The logic follows then that what is good for employees is also good for business.

When organizations and HR leaders make decisions that are at odds with what is good for employees, the long-term negative implications are far greater than the short-term gains. For example, underpaying a talented employee simply because this option is available can breed resentment, resulting in less effort from the individual. Eventually, such practices can lead to the skilled person's early resignation, accompanied by a negative Glassdoor review that can cost the organization far more in lost candidates than the cost of fair pay.

HR departments need to be reimagined to put people first in all they do. They must nurture the workforce to best serve the company's immediate and long-term goals. In doing so, employers and other organizational stakeholders "win" as much as employees.

We've explored how diversity and inclusion is changing worker expectations about the employer-employee relationship, and how the automation of HR work is threatening the existence of the HR discipline. HR professionals find themselves at a crossroads: As smart talent analytics reduces the need for HR in the future, HR professionals could easily retreat into the profession of compliance monitors. To alter this possibility, HR must step up as a change agent and become a disruptive force for good.

The change starts from within and will require restructuring HR to more aptly anticipate and respond to the needs of tomorrow's workers. The workforce of the future will be comprised of individuals with very different needs and approaches to work, working side-by-side with machines, requiring rapidly evolving skills and abilities.

Changing Leadership

No true movement towards resonance will happen without leaders who seek a new way to guide people. Understanding the current state of personal leadership and imagining what it can become are the first steps towards creating resonance.

What is the definition of "great leadership"? One proven leader—Lieutenant General George Flynn, U.S. Marine Corps, (Retired)—has the answer. George is the inspiration for a book by Simon Sinek, who interviewed him to discover more about the Marine Corps' style of leadership. George summarized it in three words—"Officers eat last." Sinek eventually named the book *Leaders Eat Last*, and George explains why.

"It's really pretty simple," he says. "If you treat your team as the most important resource in your organization, they become committed to you and the purpose of the organization. It shows your respect and the fact that you care so much about them that they deserve only the best. That includes eating first, beginning with the most junior officer and ending with the most senior officer," he says. "That's the 'cost of leadership,' as I explained it to Simon."

This leadership philosophy seems at odds with today's corporate guidance. Few CEOs know the names of many employees other than their direct reports. Many of them eat with other senior executives in a separate part of the company cafeteria and have large offices away from the rest of their employees. Certainly, this is not a "leaders eat last" approach, but one that prioritizes rank—people separated based on perceived value and contributions to the success of the organization.

There is a shift happening in some companies where CEOs are forgoing offices for shared office space, and the impact is significant for employees. "Whoever is leading must form trusted relationships with those being led," George says. "Today's generation of employees tends to demand more from its leaders. They want to know the 'why' before they buy into the project, he says. "When they believe in the value of what needs to be done, they're very giving of their time and effort. They'll go the extra mile if they understand the purpose behind the tasks and believe in that purpose."

Without this understanding, millennials (and, ultimately, all employees) are more likely to search for new employment. To retain employees, HR and other leaders must ensure they provide meaningful work that leads to the development of new skills. "Millennials need to be trained and empowered to take risks on behalf of the organization, to progress in their careers," George says.

How can today's business leaders, particularly those at the helm of large, geographically-dispersed organizations, ensure full buy-in from their "troops"? George thinks there are specific times on any given day when a leader can demonstrate valued leadership. "We call them 'defining moments,'" he says. "The moments differ, but examples include how the person makes a difficult decision or handles a mistake. Word of mouth quickly spreads to form an opinion about the leader."

These opinions form the foundation for following a leader. "In my experience, I've come across three levels of leadership," says George. "The first is when people follow you because you've been given the authority to control them. The second is when they follow you because they trust you and will, therefore, take risks for you. The third level is when they follow you because they believe in you and your mission. At that level, they'll make personal sacrifices for you. Deep down, all people want to be part of something bigger than themselves."

Leading a Reinvented Workforce

The underlying dynamics of people-centered workplace structures have definitively changed. A reinvented workforce requires new definitions and forms of leadership. Today, people willingly move from one team-based project to another, collecting new skills during these migrations. Project leaders need to create structures that accept the reality of different types of creative talents, identifying each member's unique skills sets to create optimal teams.

In building this structure, leaders must be open to others' unique differences. Each person brings a different instrument to the orchestra. To encourage the free expression of creative ideas, leaders must be facilitators and not hand out orders. Otherwise, a leader may become an anchor slowing the speed of change.

The best leaders tend to be nurturers of talent. "People don't leave companies, they leave managers." This statement has been floating around HR circles for decades—and for good reason. Employees experience work and the culture of the organization primarily through interactions with direct managers. But, people don't want to be "managed"; they want leaders who inspire and challenge them to greatness, communicate openly with them, and coach them to be their best selves at work.

Looking ahead, I expect that more companies will invest in transforming managers into leaders. As new diagnostic and prescriptive analytics tools emerge to support manager development on a daily basis, a new era of humanized people "management" can begin in earnest.

Becoming an Approachable Leader

The notion of an approachable leader that inspires, challenges, and develops others is a more recent construct in our culture and our history. Traditionally the military model of leadership—of a leader who will sacrifice his or her life for followers, thereby earning extraordinary loyalty from team members—has been most pervasive. Yet, there are multiple instances where this definition of leadership has been abused.

For example, some leaders are paid extremely well and have been provided with substantial benefits, but they spend little of their time with people in the organization, including their direct reports. In some cases, HR structures have reinforced the idea that a leader's responsibility is to make decisions for people, assign them tasks, prioritize work, and then evaluate performance. This notion ties an employee's opportunity for a promotion to their success in executing work tasks or simply "managing up" in the hierarchy.

This concept runs counter to how employees feel about the work they perform. Many employees believe they will gain more experience and opportunities through diverse work and by changing jobs, which in turn will lead to better pay and more interesting work. Doling out tasks to employees and then evaluating them on their performance does not support individuals looking to develop themselves. When people feel support for their development, however, they will contribute their energies to the organization in ways that leaders may not have imagined were possible.

Both managers and employees say the most important criteria for a leader is approachability, according research conducted by the Center for Generational Kinetics for Ultimate Software. A manager who is sits in an office behind a closed door is the antithesis of "approachable." An employee will hesitate in knocking on the door, concerned the action will be perceived as an interruption. This is no longer a valid structure in the workplace—not if approachability is the basis of the relationship. An approachable person is someone with whom team members feel comfortable asking questions and soliciting feedback.

Leaders are approachable when they listen to the voice of their employees (VoE). By developing strong relationships with employees, leaders are better able to discern whether or not they are learning and maximizing their work experiences. They need to be open to employee concerns, to coach them and make adjustments to workflows when needed. They must empower employees to freely reach across organizational lines to get work done. And they must provide clear feedback based on each person's performance, with ideas for improvement. Obviously, this is a very different type of leader.

What if Leaders Don't Adapt?

The move towards resonance requires a full, honest and reflective evaluation of the state of leadership throughout the organization. After all, modern leadership is much more than leading people toward operational results with decisiveness; it also requires a person who is approachable, inspiring, and empathetic.

If leaders don't change their traditional approach, they run the risk of losing skilled talent on their teams and throughout the organization. The reason is clear—people want leaders who listen to and understand their goals and motivations. The leaders who take thoughtful actions on behalf of their employees will attract and retain the best people who contribute fully to their team results and impact. Such leaders tend to create teams of people who express themselves openly and feel safe to challenge, create, interact, and collaborate—inside and outside the boundaries of the traditional organization to the benefit of the organization and the entire workforce.

The impact of having unapproachable leaders who simply manage people instead of relating to them is dramatic. Fear infiltrates the workplace, with the outcome of people spending more time covering their bases than working and innovating.

What if Organizations Don't Evolve?

The method and pace at which any organization adapts its culture and practices to develop resonance with the workforce is a matter of choice. But, it is no longer a choice to ignore the fact that work structures need to be revisited and likely revised. Otherwise, companies risk losing their best talent, impact their ability to attract and replace people, and decrease employee productivity and bottom line value. Of course, not everyone can job hop; there are location and other forms of constraint for some people. An organization won't necessarily lose all its top talent, not immediately. But, why take the chance?

To attract and retain the best people, business leaders and HR need to create a work environment where people truly like to come to work, feel they are contributing, and believe they have a purpose. These feelings will make them more productive and fulfilled. A healthy, motivated workforce is a productive one.

One Step at a Time

Even in very large organizations, listening to the voice of your employees, understanding what's most important to them, and then beginning to make incremental changes that take these messages to heart is a critical step towards resonance.

Starting small is important, given the disruption that may occur by committing to massive changes, such as publicly announcing that the company will be overhauling the entire culture. This would result not in long-term resonance, but in short-term dissonance.

After completing this fact-finding mission, analyze the organization's culture—how the planned changes will align with the context and authentic "self" of the organization. Each organization has a unique history and set of traditions; therefore it is crucial to be mindful of these cultural elements while moving forward. Continue to assess the organization's culture and then contemplate how it may need to change in the future. I refer to this as "Culture Casting," and it has three components:

- Make an honest appraisal of the current culture—casting a bright spotlight on it.
- Identify the culture's "cast of characters" —the different people within the organization—to understand what drives them and what impact they have on the culture.
- Project and communicate a vision of the ideal culture the organization seeks. It is particularly important to include employees when formulating this future to ensure a vision that is authentic, realistic, and addresses perception gaps between leaders and employees.

Planning for Outcomes

Following the completion of these steps, ask the following questions:

- Do we need to flatten the organization?
- Do we want to create fluid work groups, forming to tackle specific problems, then dispersing and reforming again based on organizational needs?
- Do we need to create multiple representations of our organization to better communicate the value of the organization for our teams?
- Does the structure match the way our organization operates, or does it impede work getting done?
- Do we want to allow teams to form themselves?
- Do we want to rethink how we transfer people and accomplish reorganizations, by reaching out to people to learn more about what work motivates and interests them before making a change?
- Should we allow people to choose to work together, based on the trust established within that group?

There are literally an endless number of places to begin, but begin you must.

Finding Your Champions and Resources

When looking for allies in launching a resonant workplace, do not limit the search to current managers or executives. Open the movement towards resonance to a broader group of people; otherwise, the natural frequencies of people “in the moment” and some of the most inspiring individual contributors may be overlooked.

While it may seem counterintuitive to achieve significant change without an equally significant resource investment, resonance does not require a large budget and massive people resources. As you communicate what you are doing, people will be motivated to assist your efforts to make the organization resonant. They will help identify what resonates and what does not. They will also be eager to adjust their behavior to achieve greater transparency and communication to do what is necessary to bring about resonance. The journey is a joint one to be taken together—workforce and workplace.

Find and support individuals who step up to ensure they have the space and time to advocate resonance as vocal champions. Reward them in the form of face time with other leaders advocating for resonance. Do not be deterred by people who are not on board with the journey towards resonance.

Be sure to identify an inspiring, innovative person to lead the charge, someone not likely to be disheartened by setbacks and naysayers. Strive to create frequent, open communication and checkpoints with champions. When you decide a formal initiative is needed, ensure it is nimble and always inclusive, as the goal is an engaged and productive workforce.

Here's another piece of advice: Think about one thing discussed in this book that can change your organization in the next six months to a year. Then, analyze this change by comparing it to the current state. The stories that follow will provide a glimpse into experiences of resonance that may inspire you on your own journey.

CHAPTER 8: RESONANCE ACHIEVED

A Reimagined Future of Work

Employees today want meaningful work lives and productive careers. As we have explored, this puts the onus on employers to transform the workplace as part of a person's work experience. Companies that listen to these demands and create a more open workplace, run by approachable leaders who embrace each person's uniqueness, will have greater opportunities to recruit and retain the best people. In such workplaces, everyone will feel free to fully express themselves and contribute to the organization in purposeful ways.

What might this new workplace and new workforce experiences look like? Here are potential manifestations of resonance achieved.

Specialists and Free Agents

For people with sought-after specialized skills, the gig economy opens a new world of possibilities. Specialized skills will become increasingly scarce and competition for those skills will be fierce. These individuals will have the option of providing their services on contract terms for a period of time. They will eventually become so ubiquitous and valuable that an industry of "agents" will emerge to represent them. While the independent contractor will secure and pay their agents, some organizations may decide to absorb agent commissions or fees as a means of competing for the best talent.

Agents may also provide professional and personal development assistance to their clients, possibly advocating for the employee to ensure a positive work experience. They may further become involved in employment-related conflict resolution, requiring a shift in mindset for HR leaders to work with these employee advocates. Lastly, the number of independent contractors may increase in the future as college graduates engage in agent relationships before entering the workforce.

Company-Focused Generalists

Alternatively, many people will want the financial security and long-term collaborations provided in a more traditional work arrangement, in which salaried employees stay with a single organization for as long as feasible. However, their expectations will differ than those of the traditional "company man" of the 1960s.

Such employees will seek opportunities to change the focus of their work frequently, to consistently cultivate their aptitudes. In response, employers will need to develop flexible teams more focused on the nature of work than on jobs or positions. They will need to continually develop new work challenges for salaried employees to engage their interest, contributing to the organization's success.

Tomorrow's workplace also will place less emphasis on seniority. Just as inexperienced rookies can make more money than veteran players on a sports team, organizations will pay a premium for talent and potential. As a result, the vetting process will become more sophisticated and data-driven. Both generalist and specialist workers will want similar things, including an increasing scope and variety of challenges, responsibilities and rewards, and the ability to reach their potential and dreams.

HR Departments of the Future

The way each group of employees goes about achieving their work and career goals creates very different implications for business leaders and HR departments. There is little question that what can be automated will be automated. Rather than self-service tools that require employees to take action, IT systems will become more interactive and highly personalized. These systems will be based on continuous feedback and the analysis of a new class of "interaction" data, created by people through their use of systems and machines.

By analyzing this data, companies will fine-tune systems to provide work experiences that help people achieve their aspirations. Such work experience solutions will give people greater control over their careers and enrich HR's understanding of employees. (The Jensen Group, Reimagining HR for the Augmented Age, 2018). By the same token, what can be augmented through the use of AI, robotics, and other workforce productivity and efficiency tools should be augmented, with this caveat: while HR will use AI in performing workforce analyses, HR must also continually enhance the value of these analyses by developing new questions and providing invaluable context for the findings.

For that reason, HR professionals in the future will be people scientists with keen insights into human behavior and motivation. By understanding big data, they will draw people-related insights that will impact their organizations' short-term and long-term performance. HR professionals will become relationship brokers between managers and their reports, between peers looking to facilitate communication, and across departments. In this process, they will advance the criticality of D&I toward attaining business success, as the world of work becomes more globally diverse and the need for inclusiveness increases.

The HR function will need to be rethought and reorganized to support these goals. More explicitly, the experiences of people will become even more of a primary responsibility as others have, such as compliance and workforce productivity. As this shift occurs, HR professionals will have to become comfortable relegating back-stage functions of compliance and productivity analyses to automation and AI, with assistance from their organization's data scientists. The future will entail a focus on a wider scope of critical human-led initiatives and interactions, augmented at times with AI.

Such a structure will make HR more proactive in uncovering and addressing future challenges, and nimble in responding to changes in direction. The most important aspect of this new role is person-centricity, the ability to understand, predict, and respond to human behavior, and translate this understanding into positive action that fulfills the potential of people and ensures organizational success.

Looking further ahead, HR professionals will have two clearly-defined role choices. For instance, they may choose to become advocates for the organization, fully responsible for developing the workforce to best serve its immediate and long-term goals. Such organization-focused HR professionals would be experts in the workings of organizational success, creating new initiatives and opportunities that help employees become their most effective while inspiring to perform at their best.

By creating best practice strategies for working with a fluid global workforce, introducing new open-door policies, developing short-term benefits for giggers, and nurturing leaders to quickly and deeply connect with diverse work teams, such HR leaders would usher in a new era of organizational design.

These Organizational HR Advocates would work closely with a second defined HR role—the People Agent. This new HR professional role would unabashedly and without compromise advocate for employees, without being beholden to the organization for their livelihood. People Agents would do much more than simply negotiate pay increases and new salary terms; for instance, they could advocate for an individual employee experiencing conflict on a team. Ideally, such HR professionals would have lasting relationships with employees, spanning many years and multiple job postings.

The choice of a People Agent would be left to employees. In this model, each employee, regardless of role, could have an individual People Agent funded by the person via compensation withholding or by the organization itself. With regard to the latter, companies may be incented to pay for People Agent fees, given that People Agents may help attract and represent superior talent, by demonstrating trust and the importance of unbiased employee advocacy.

The lasting and personal nature of the relationship between employees and People Agents differentiates it from labor union advocacy. Organizations would have to become more open—almost borderless—in this reimagined future, so that the interventions of "outsider" People Agents on behalf of the employees they represent could succeed.

In the end, the gains would be balanced for all parties: Employees gain greater control of their work destinies and ensure they are well represented at work, and organizations gain more satisfied, engaged, and motivated employees performing at their best, knowing they are valued and fully supported. For HR to achieve such dual responsibilities, they must feel empowered to "call the meeting" with business leaders rather than wait for an invitation to sit at the proverbial table, to demonstrate to executive leaders the inextricable link between people success and business success.

Resonance is possible for all organizations, but it takes work. At the beginning of this book, I mentioned that every change needs to start with a vision—an aspirational picture of a desired future state. The fictitious stories that follow paint a picture of what life could be like when a workplace and its people are in resonance.

A Resonant Worklife Story: Cassandra

Cassandra has been working as an hourly employee for a construction company, Dream Builders, preparing new project estimates for the past three months. She's excited about the work, but is always looking for new challenges to develop her skills, browsing short and long-term work and projects on the company's open opportunity dashboard and kiosk. In her spare time, Cassandra follows her creative passion working as a professional photographer, making her a participant in the gig economy.

In her primary job, she meets bi-weekly with her People Agent, who understands the organization and advocates for Cassandra as she navigates job opportunities. Cassandra contracted with the People Agent prior to her college graduation. At the meetings, Cassandra confides growing concerns about her team, particularly her new manager, who came on board two weeks earlier and has not yet reached out to her. She also discusses her work aspirations to be sure she is pursuing the right career growth opportunities. Cassandra feels encouraged and inspired by her People Agent, who really knows her and regularly checks in on her development.

Cassandra has also signed up to be coached by another employee at Dream Builders, someone with significant tenure at the company. She is interested in learning how employees in upper leadership navigated their career progression. This opportunity not only connects Cassandra more closely with the company, but with the perspectives of someone from a different generation. The HR Organizational Advocate—the individual who represents the organization to its employees, similar to today's HR business partners—also checks in with Cassandra regularly to ensure she has the best possible experience with her system-matched coach.

A Resonant Worklife Story: Schuyler

Schuyler is a manager at a financial firm and a recent immigrant from the Netherlands. Schuyler is genderfluid and would like team members to use they/their/them pronouns when addressing and referring to them. But they have only been with the firm for a few weeks, and are struggling on two fronts: they need to better understand the dynamics of their new team, and they have a personal issue they need to discuss with someone at the firm before introducing it to the team.

Schuyler reaches out to their HR Organizational Advocate and gets the lay of land with their team in more detail. The HROA offers them institutional knowledge, and also the chance to ask their team some open-ended questions, using a perceptive feedback system to understand more about their current sentiments and moods. Together, Schuyler and the HROA move on to discussing Schuyler's genderfluidity and interest in the team's use of they/their/them pronouns. They seek advice on when to share it with the team. The HROA helps them put together a plan of action that includes letting their own leader know about the change.

The HROA also helps Schuyler know what to expect in terms of company policies, profile update processes, and communication expectations. Schuyler feels completely at ease, goes to the life event page on the company's website to make the change directly, and receives recommendations about community and company support resources.

A Resonant Worklife Story: James

James is an engineer at ABC Inc. who has been having trouble with a new team member. The person presented herself very well during the team interview, but now seems overconfident and is getting all the best programming assignments and other projects. James believes his manager unfairly favors the new employee, who is an African-American woman, because of the manager's interest in promoting diversity.

He decides to set up a meeting between his People Agent and the manager to discuss the situation. James's manager, Nina, calls upon the HR Organizational Advocate to be part of this meeting to discuss the importance of having diverse representation on the team and how "intersectional difference" (when someone is a member of multiple underrepresented groups) can compound feelings of exclusion for people. James comes away with a better understanding of the real reason why the new employee's unique skillset and experience at other organizations is giving her the best assignments.

The meeting also gives James the opportunity to share what kind of work is particularly interesting and important to him. As a follow-up, Nina and James' People Agent agree to check back in regularly to ensure he is given a chance to work on choice project assignments. The HROA works with Nina to connect James and the new employee in a shared work experience, with the goal of increasing his acceptance and appreciation of different perspectives at work.

A Resonant Division Closure Story: WidgiCorp Inc.

WidgiCorp Inc. is a multinational robotic widget company with multiple divisions including research, manufacturing, retail outlets and partner distribution and sales. Because the organization operates in many countries, WidgiCorp has adopted formal cultural awareness and inclusion training initiatives for employees. People are encouraged to audition and apply for assignments across divisions to keep them engaged, energized, and continuously developing. Leaders frequently post short-term opportunities for both salaried employees and employee-referred external gig workers on an internal marketplace to fill immediate gaps and other team needs.

Despite the company's success, external events and market disruptions have compelled the closure of a regional site, adversely affecting the jobs of hundreds of employees. Employees understand the reasons for the closure, as WidgiCorp leaders have been transparent about the business' performance and outcomes. The HROA in the impacted region activates his network of HR professionals and other business colleagues to look for work placements for the displaced individuals.

The employees' professional and personal aspirations are documented in their many feedback meetings with business supervisors and other leaders at WidgiCorp. To determine next steps, they are invited to join working groups within or outside of the company. WidgiCorp has formed a collaborative community of business peers (some might call them competitors) to help ensure minimal employment impact from a business or market disruption.

By the time the regional operation closes its doors, all affected employees have been relocated or have new work placements outside the company. Some have been helped to find satisfactory gig work, thanks to the company's proactive efforts. A few have had to adapt rapidly to dramatically different types of work, but WidgiCorp's practice of requiring first-year employees to be part of flex team rotations has helped prepare them for the change. Moreover, since employees were included in discussions about their future, they were better able to plan for worst-case scenarios. This open, collaborative preparation with the employer has given each employee control over their destiny and a future, despite the tough business decisions needed.

These fictitious scenarios demonstrate the importance of deeply understanding what drives people's behaviors and choices at work, and its relationship to becoming a resonant workplace. While the time and effort may seem significant, new technologies can lighten the load, helping leaders, advocates and employees by processing and analyzing comments and emotions and recommending actions.

Nothing completely replaces human interaction. But newer ways of leading, and the use of technology to listen to the needs, hopes and anxieties of employees, can help companies scale to better serve people, moving organizations forward synchronously toward greater success. Having achieved resonance, businesses earn an enviable name in the talent marketplace, have contented workers within their organizations, and become part of a network of past and future workers willing to publicly promote the organization's excellent treatment of people.

You Are Doing the Right Thing

If you are reading this book, you are a person with a passion for your people and your organization. If nothing else, I hope you have come away knowing that things are changing and that you can make a difference.

I wish you all the best on your journey and would welcome the chance to discuss your experiences. I can be reached at resonance.thebook@gmail.com.

NOTES

CHAPTER 1:
WHAT IS RESONANCE? 1

How Millennials Want to Work & Live; The Six Big Changes Leaders have to Make, Gallup, 2016

2017 Deloitte Global Human Capital Trends; Rewriting the rules for the digital age

Planning Your Post-Retirement Career, Dorie Clark, Harvard Business Review, April 28, 2016

Finances in Retirement, New Challenges, New Solutions - Bank of America Merrill Lynch survey in partnership with New Age, 2017

CHAPTER 2:
HOW WE GOT HERE 11

Testimony of Frederick W. Taylor at hearings before Special Committee of the House of Representatives, January, 1912: Taylor Society, 1926

The Ford Century, Russ Banham, Workman Books, 2002.

Pros and Cons: Advantages of Telecommuting for the Community, a Meta-analysis by Global Workplace Analytics, 2015

A motivation expert explains why businesses go about motivating people all wrong — and how to do it better, Chris Weller, Business Insider, January 12, 2017.

National Study on Satisfaction at Work, The Center for Generational Kinetics and Ultimate Software, 2016

HR Forecast Study, Crain's New York, March 2018

Trends in Employee Recognition, World at Work, Underwritten by ITA Group, May 2017

State of the American Workplace, Gallup, 2017

State of the Global Workplace, Gallup, 2017

CHAPTER 3:
DISSONANCE EXPOSED 21

The Benefits of Diversity & Inclusion Initiatives, Russ Banham, Risk Management, June 1, 2018

Women in the Workplace 2016, September, 2016. A study conducted by LeanIn.Org and McKinsey

Women in the Workplace 2018 – September, 2018. A study conducted by LeanIn.Org and McKinsey

Women and Leadership; Public Says Women are Equally Qualified, but Barriers Persist, Pew Research Center, January 14, 2015

Pew Research Center survey, Nov 12-21, 2014 (N + 1,835)

Women: Work and Life Well-Lived: How to Attract, Engage, and Retain a Gender-Diverse Workforce – Gallup, 2016

These are the only women CEOs left among S&P 500 companies, Lauren Thomas, CNBC, August 6, 2018

The New York Times Glass Ceiling Index, inspired by an EY Center for Board Matters report, Women on US boards: what are we seeing?, 2018

The Top Jobs Where Women Are Outnumbered by Men Named John, NYT, The Upshots, April 24, 2018

Why is Silicon Valley So Awful to Women? Liza Mundy, The Atlantic, April, 2017 issue

Elephant in The Valley, 2015: The Elephant in the Valley is a collaborative effort between seven women in Silicon

Valley with backgrounds including Venture Capital, Academia, Entrepreneurship, Product Marketing and Marketing Research

Three Reminders Women in Technology Need to Hear, Anitab.org Insights, 2017

Survey Led by Rosenbluth Sheds New Light on Women's Issues in Workforce, Alison Coleman, Yale University, Faculty of Arts and Sciences, April 10, 2017

Women in The Global Workforce, A Survey of Students and Alumni of the Business Schools in the Global Network for Advanced Management, Frances Rosenbluth, Gareth Nellis, and Michael Weaver, March 2017

US Dep't of Labor, Software Developers, Systems Software: Percent of Women Employed (2011); U.S. Census Bureau* * Note: The percentages for employment by gender come from the 2011 American Community Survey (ACS)

Does Race Matter in Neighborhood Preferences? Results from a Video Experiment, Maria Krysan, Couper, Reynolds Farley, and Tyrone Forman, US National Library of Medicine, National Institutes of Health. Author manuscript; available in PMC 2013 Jul 8. Published in final edited form as: AJS. 2009 Sep; 115(2): 527–559. PMCID: PMC3704191, NIHMSID: NIHMS482504, PMID: 20614764

Finding Work When You're On the Autism Spectrum: It Could Be an Advantage, US News & World Report, May 30,2017

Autism Speaks – autismspeaks.org/employment

Stigma: Alive and well, American Psychological Association, Sadie F. Dingfelder, June 2009 (Vol. 40, No. 6)

Of Fear and Loathing: The role of "disturbing behavior," labels, and causal attributions in shaping public attitudes toward people with mental illness. Martin, J.K. Percosolido, B.A., & Tuch, S.A. (2000). Journal of Health and Social Behavior, 41, 208-223 (Vol. 41, No. 2).

Autism Can Be An Asset In The Workplace, Employers And Workers Find, NPR, May 18. 2016

Open Office, Susan Dominus, New York Times, February, 2019

Winning personality: The advantages of being an ambivert, Meghan Holohan, Today, Feb. 8, 2016

Rethinking the Extraverted Sales Ideal: The Ambivert Advantage, Adam M. Grant First Published April 8, 2013 Research

"Why America's Black Mothers and Babies Are in a Life-or-Death Crisis" – Linda Villarose, NYT, April 11, 2018

Quick Take: Lesbian, Gay, Bisexual and Transgender Workplace Issues, Catalyst, June 06, 2018

The Gay and Transgender Wage Gap, Center for American Progress, Crosby Burns, April 16, 2012 - via The Williams Institute UCLA School of Law

Sexual orientation and disclosure in relation to psychiatric symptoms, diurnal cortisol, and allostatic load. Juster RP, Smith NG, Ouellet É, Sindi S, Lupien SJ. Psychosom Med. 2013 Feb;75(2):103-16. doi: 10.1097/PSY.0b013e3182826881. Epub 2013 Jan 29.
David M. Huebner, Ph.D., M.P.H. Mary C. Davis, Ph.D.

Gay and bisexual men who disclose their sexual orientations in the workplace have higher workday levels of salivary cortisol and negative affect, *Annals of Behavioral Medicine*, Volume 30, Issue 3, 1 December 2005, Pages 260–267

Stigma and diurnal cortisol among transitioning transgender men. Robert-Paul Juster, L. Zachary DuBois, Bethany G Everett, Sally Powers, Poster (PDF Available) in Psychoneuroendocrinology 71:51 · September 2016

CHAPTER 4:
GIGS, LATERALS AND STRETCH ASSIGNMENTS 47

CONTINGENT WORKFORCE: Size, Characteristics, Earnings, and Benefits. GAO-15-168R: Published: Apr 20, 2015. Publicly Released: May 20, 2015.

How Much Does An Employee Cost? Starting Up: Practical Advice for Entrepreneurs, Joseph G. Hadzima Jr., MIT Sloan School of Management; Reprint from the Monthly Column in the Boston Business Journal, 1994-2005

Workplace 2025: from employer to contributor: the worker of the future, Randstad USA, 2017

The New Total Workforce, Russ Banham, HRO, April 12, 2016

CHAPTER 5:
BEYOND AUTOMATION 59

Whopping 3.9 billion people are now using the Internet, Check this UN report, By: AFP | Published: December 7, 2018

The Fourth Industrial Revolution: what it means, how to respond, Klaus Schwab, World Economic Forum, January 14, 2016

Future of Jobs Report 2018, The World Economic Forum, September 17, 2018

The Rise Of The Freelancer Economy, Brian Rashid, Forbes, January 26, 2016

Intuit: Gig economy is 34% of US workforce, Patrick Gillespie, CNNMoney, May 24, 2017

Workplace 2025: from employer to contributor: the worker of the future, Randstad USA, 2017

Workforce 2025; the future of the world of work, Randstad Canada, 2016

Intuit 2020 Report; Twenty Trends That Will Shape the Next Decade, Intuit, October 2010

Machines Taught by Photos Learn a Sexist View of Women, Tom Simonite, Wired, August 21, 2017

Adversarial Removal of Gender from Deep Image Representations, Tianlu Wang, Jieyu Zhao, Mark Yatskar, Kai-Wei Chang, Vicente Ordonez. arXiv:1811.08489. November 2018.

AI 100: The Artificial Intelligence Startups Redefining Industries, CB Insights, February 6, 2019

Why countries need to work together on AI, Ganesh Bell, World Economic Forum, September 16, 2018

CHAPTER 6:
THE BELONGING IMPERATIVE 77

Microsoft's Mission to Empower All Extends Beyond Technology, Mary Bailey, HuffPost, 07/10/2017; Updated August 16, 2017

Diversity and inclusion update: The journey continues, Lindsay-Rae McIntyre, Chief Diversity Officer, Microsoft, November 14, 2018

Implicit Racial/Ethnic Bias Among Health Care Professionals and Its Influence on Health Care Outcomes: A Systematic Review, Am J Public Health. William J. Hall, PhD, Mimi V. Chapman, PhD, Kent M. Lee, MS, Yesenia M. Merino, MPH, Tainayah W. Thomas, MPH, B. Keith Payne, PhD, Eugenia Eng, DrPH, Steven H. Day, MCP, and Tamera Coyne-Beasley, MD, 2015, US National Library of Medicine, National Institutes of Health. December, 2015; 105(12): e60–e76. Published online. doi: 10.2105/AJPH.2015.302903, PMCID: PMC4638275, PMID: 26469668

The Implicit Association Test (IAT), Yale, 1998

CHAPTER 7:
MOVING TOWARDS RESONANCE 89

State of the Global Workplace, Gallup, 2017

The Historical Background Of Human Resource Management, VinayKumar S, October 12, 2015, LinkedIn

Reimaging HR for the Augmented Age, Ultimate Software/ The Jensen Group, 2018

Uncovering the Positive Drivers of Employee Experience, The Center for Generational Kinetics and Ultimate Software, 2017

Culture Casting, Cecile Alper-Leroux, Ultimate Software, 2017

CHAPTER 8:
RESONANCE ACHIEVED 113

Reimaging HR for the Augmented Age, Ultimate Software/ The Jensen Group, 2018